JONAH
and
MICAH

J. Vernon McGee

THOMAS NELSON
Since 1798

NASHVILLE   DALLAS   MEXICO CITY   RIO DE JANEIRO

Published in Nashville, Tennessee, by Thomas Nelson, Inc.

Scripture quotations are from the KING JAMES VERSION of the Bible.

Library of Congress Cataloging-in-Publication Data

McGee, J. Vernon (John Vernon), 1904–1988
    [Thru the Bible with J. Vernon McGee]
    Thru the Bible commentary series / J. Vernon McGee.
        p.   cm.
    Reprint. Originally published: Thru the Bible with J. Vernon
McGee. 1975.
    Includes bibliographical references.
    ISBN 0-7852-1032-6 (TR)
    ISBN 0-7852-1091-1 (NRM)
    1. Bible—Commentaries. I. Title.
BS491.2.M37   1991
220.7'7—dc20   90–41340
ISBN: 978-0-7852-0573-9   CIP

Printed in the United States

25 QG 14 13

CONTENTS

JONAH

MICAH

PREFACE

The radio broadcasts of the Thru the Bible Radio five-year program were transcribed, edited, and published first in single-volume paperbacks to accommodate the radio audience.

There has been a minimal amount of further editing for this publication. Therefore, these messages are not the word-for-word recording of the taped messages which went out over the air. The changes were necessary to accommodate a reading audience rather than a listening audience.

These are popular messages, prepared originally for a radio audience. They should not be considered a commentary on the entire Bible in any sense of that term. These messages are devoid of any attempt to present a theological or technical commentary on the Bible. Behind these messages is a great deal of research and study in order to interpret the Bible from a popular rather than from a scholarly (and too-often boring) viewpoint.

We have definitely and deliberately attempted "to put the cookies on the bottom shelf so that the kiddies could get them."

The fact that these messages have been translated into many languages for radio broadcasting and have been received with enthusiasm reveals the need for a simple teaching of the whole Bible for the masses of the world.

I am indebted to many people and to many sources for bringing this volume into existence. I should express my especial thanks to my secretary, Gertrude Cutler, who supervised the editorial work; to Dr. Elliott R. Cole, my associate, who handled all the detailed work with the publishers; and finally, to my wife Ruth for tenaciously encouraging me from the beginning to put my notes and messages into printed form.

Solomon wrote, ". . . of making many books there is no end; and much study is a weariness of the flesh" (Eccl. 12:12). On a sea of books that flood the marketplace, we launch this series of THRU THE BIBLE with the hope that it might draw many to the one Book, *The Bible*.

J. VERNON MCGEE

Jonah

The Book of

JONAH

INTRODUCTION

Jonah is the book of the Bible which perhaps has been criticized more than any other. Unfortunately, many Christians thoughtlessly cast aspersions upon this important book in the canon of Scripture without realizing that they are playing into the hands of the critics and innocently becoming the dupes of the skeptics. You hear even Christians say, when they hear a tall story, "My, that's a Jonah!" What they really mean is that it is something that is hard, or maybe even impossible, to believe.

In warfare the tactic of the enemy is always to feel out the weak spot in the line of the opposition and to center his attack at that vantage point. Judging by this criterion, many critics have evidently come to the conclusion that the Book of Jonah is the vulnerable part of the divine record. This book is the spot where the enemy has leveled his heaviest artillery. As a result, the average Christian today feels that this is the weakest of the sixty-six links in the chain of the Scriptures. If this link gives away, then the chain is broken.

Is the Book of Jonah "the Achilles' heel" of the Bible? It is if we are to accept the ridiculous explanations of the critics. The translators of the Septuagint were the first to question the reasonableness of this book. They set the pattern for the avalanche of criticism which has come down to the present day. The ancient method of modernism is to allegorize the book and to classify it with *Robinson Crusoe* and *Gulliver's Travels*. Today liberalism uses the same tactics. They make of it an allegory, saying that actually it never took place at all.

Some of the extravagant theories of the critics are so farfetched and fantastic that they are almost ridiculous. It is much easier to believe the Book of Jonah as given than to believe their explanations of it. I would like to pass on to you some of these outlandish explanations of the Book of Jonah:

1. Some critics, without a scrap of evidence to support their claim, say that Jonah was the son of the widow of Zarephath.

2. There are some who have put forth the theory that Jonah had a dream in the ship while he was asleep during the storm and that the Book of Jonah is the account of his dream.

3. Some relate the Book of Jonah to the Phoenician myth of Hercules and the sea monster. There is no similarity at all and, again, they are reaching for an explanation.

4. Another group holds that, although Jonah was a real character and did take a ship to Tarshish, a storm wrecked the ship. Then after the storm and shipwreck, Jonah was picked up by another ship on which there was a fish for its figurehead, and that gives support for the record in the Book of Jonah. I can well understand that if Jonah had been picked up after the storm, he might have been unconscious for awhile. I can also imagine that he might have felt like he was in a fish at that time. But I'm of the opinion that after recovering, on about the second day, Jonah would have come to the conclusion that he was on a ship and not inside a fish!

5. Still others resort to the wild claim that there was a dead fish floating around and that Jonah took refuge in it during the storm. This group has a dead fish and a live Jonah. Before we are through with this book, I am going to turn it around and say that what we have is a live fish and a dead Jonah.

Therefore, liberalism largely takes the position that the Book of Jonah is nothing in the world but an allegory, that it is merely a fairy story to be put in the same category as *Aesop's Fables*. The producers of these speculations claim that the Book of Jonah is unreasonable, and they bring forth these theories to give credence to their story. It would be very interesting indeed to get Jonah's reactions to their "very reasonable" explanations.

We must dismiss all of these speculations as having no basis in fact, no vestige of proof from a historical standpoint, and as having existence only in the imaginations of the critics. It can be established that Jonah was an historical person, not a character from mythology. It can be ascertained on good authority that the account is accurate. And it can be shown that the message of the book is of utmost significance even for this crucial time in which we live.

Jonah is an historical character and the author of this book. I want to turn to an historical book, 2 Kings, where we read: "In the fifteenth year of Amaziah the son of Joash king of Judah Jeroboam the son of Joash king of Israel began to reign in Samaria, and reigned forty and one years" (2 Kings 14:23). As far as I know, no one has ever questioned that Jeroboam II lived, that he was a king in the northern kingdom of Israel, and that he reigned forty-one years. This is an historical record. We read further: "And he did that which was evil in the sight of the LORD: he departed not from all the sins of Jeroboam the son of Nebat, who made Israel to sin. He restored the coast of Israel from the entering of Hamath unto the sea of the plain, according to the word of the LORD God of Israel, which he spake by the hand of his servant, *Jonah, the son of Amittai, the prophet, which was of Gath-hepher*" (2 Kings 14:24–25, italics mine). Jeroboam was a real person, Israel was a real nation, Hamath was a real place, and it is quite unlikely that this man Jonah is a figment of the imagination. This is an historical record, and it is reasonable to conclude that Jonah is an historical character.

It is begging the point to say that this is *another* Jonah. It is not reasonable to believe that there were two Jonahs whose fathers were named Amittai and who were both prophets. This is especially evident when it is observed that the name of Jonah was not a common name; after all, Jonah is not like our American surname of Jones! The only times that the name occurs in the Bible are in this reference in 2 Kings, in the Book of Jonah itself, and in the New Testament references to that book. There is only one Jonah in the Bible, and he is an historical person.

It is quite interesting in this regard to compare the case of Jonah with another of the prophets, Obadiah. As far as I know, no critic has ever questioned the existence of a man by the name of Obadiah who wrote the Book of Obadiah; yet there is not one historical record in either the Old or New Testament concerning Obadiah. The liberals accept Obadiah, but they reject Jonah. Why? Because they want to deny the miracle that is recorded here.

We have an historical record of Jonah in the Old Testament, and we also have one in the New Testament given by the greatest authority who has ever lived on this earth, the Lord Jesus Christ. He personally gave authenticity to the historical character of Jonah and to his experience in the fish. We read in Luke 11:30, "For as Jonas was a sign unto the Ninevites, so shall also the Son of man be to this generation." Then in Matthew 12:39–41 we read: "But he answered and said unto them, An evil and adulterous generation seeketh after a sign; and there shall no sign be given to it, but the sign of the prophet Jonas: for as Jonas was three days and three nights in the whale's belly; so shall the Son of man be three days and three nights in the heart of the earth. The men of Nineveh shall rise in judgment with this generation, and shall condemn it: because they repented at the preaching of Jonas; and, behold, a greater than Jonas is here."

The moment you question the historical record of the Book of Jonah, you question the credibility of the Lord Jesus Christ. It is very strange to hear the liberal say, "Jesus was the greatest teacher that ever lived," since one of the marks of a great teacher is that what he teaches is accurate and truthful. If Jesus is a great teacher, my friend, then His authentication of the Book of Jonah has to stand.

I want to conclude this section in which I have attempted to meet the objections of the critics by quoting the late Sir Winston Churchill on the subject of the inspiration of the Scriptures:

> We reject with scorn all those learned and laboured myths that Moses was but a legendary figure upon whom the priesthood and the people hung their essential social, moral and religious ordinances. We believe that the most scientific view, the most up-to-date and rationalistic conception, will find its fullest satisfaction in taking the Bible story literally, and in identifying one of the greatest human beings with the most decisive leap forward ever discernible in the human story. We remain unmoved by the tomes of Professor Gradgrind and Dr. Dryasdust.

We may be sure that all these things happened just as they are set out according to Holy Writ.

Jonah was a prophet, but his little book is not a prophecy—that is, there is no prophecy of the future recorded in it. It is, instead, a personal account of a major event in the life of Jonah; as the narrator, he tells us his experience.

This narrative carries two great messages. We have here in miniature a picture of the nation Israel in the Great Tribulation period, a picture of how God will preserve His people, the 144,000 who are sealed in the Book of Revelation. We also have here a marvelous teaching concerning the resurrection of Jesus Christ. This book is actually prophetic of the Resurrection. The Lord Jesus Himself said that just as Jonah was a sign to the Ninevites, He also would be a sign to His generation in His resurrection from the dead.

The Book of Jonah is not a fish story, and that is something which really disturbs the gainsaying world which makes a great deal of how impossible it is to believe it. This book is a picture of a man who was raised from the dead, and of a throne in the midst of which "stood a Lamb as it had been slain." This Lamb is a resurrected Lamb, and a Christ-rejecting world will some day cry out, ". . . hide us from the face of him that sitteth on the throne, and from the wrath of the Lamb" (Rev. 6:16).

Sometimes the literary excellence of this brief brochure is lost in the din made by the carping critics. It is well to recall the tribute paid by Charles Reade, the English literary critic and author, who wrote, "Jonah is the most beautiful story ever written in so small a compass." It is well to keep in mind that we have before us a literary gem, not a fish story.

Another salient point that I want to make is that the fish is neither the hero of the story nor the villain of the story. This book is not even about a fish, although the fish does become very important. The chief difficulty is in keeping a correct perspective. The fish is merely window dressing and cake trimming. In every play there are certain props and settings. It does not really matter whether *Hamlet* is played against a black, red, blue or white backdrop—that is not the important thing. In the story of Jonah, the fish is among the props and does not occupy the star's dressing room.

In dealing with any book of the Bible, we need to distinguish between what Dr. G. Campbell Morgan calls the essentials and the incidentals. The incidentals in the Book of Jonah are the fish, the gourd, the east wind, the boat, and even the city of Nineveh. The essentials here are Jehovah and Jonah—God and man—that is what the book is all about.

Conservative scholars place the writing of the Book of Jonah before 745 B.C. The incidents took place about that time. Some even place it as early as 860 B.C. In my judgment, it seems best to place it between 800 and 750 B.C. Students of history will recognize this as the period when Nineveh, founded by Nimrod, was in its heyday, when the Assyrian nation was the great world power of the day. That nation was destroyed about 606 B.C. By the time of Herodotus, the Greek historian, the city of Nimrod had ceased to exist. When Xenophon passed the city, it was deserted, but he testified that the walls still stood and were 150 feet high. Historians now estimate they were 100 feet high and 40 feet thick. Nineveh, as we are going to see, was a great city, and we are told as much here in the record.

The brevity of the Book of Jonah is apt to lead the casual reader to the conclusion that there is nothing of particular significance here except the diatribe about the whale that swallowed Jonah. (The Greek word for whale is *kêtos*, meaning "a great sea monster." Although it could have been a whale, I do not think it was—for the Scripture tells us that a special fish was prepared.) But the Book of Jonah has four very brief chapters, and it is only a little more than twice as long as the Book of Obadiah, which is the shortest book in the Old Testament. Because it is very brief, we are apt to pass over it. However, we should not call any of these books "minor" prophets, for each is like a little atom bomb, just loaded with power and with a program of God.

There are six significant subjects which are suggested and developed in the Book of Jonah which make it very relevant for us today:

1. This is the one book of the Old Testament which sets forth *the resurrection of Jesus Christ*. All of the great doctrines of the Christian faith are set forth in certain books of the Old Testament. For instance,

the Book of Exodus sets forth redemption. The deliverance from sin for the sinner who comes to Christ is illustrated in that book. In the Book of Ruth you have the romance of redemption, the love side of redemption. In the Book of Esther, you have the romance of providence. The book of Job, I believe, teaches repentance. You can go through the Scriptures and find that the great doctrines of our faith are illustrated in various books of the Old Testament. The little Book of Jonah illustrates and teaches the resurrection of the Lord Jesus. If this book does not teach the great doctrine of resurrection, then this most important doctrine of the Christian faith is not illustrated by a book in the Old Testament. For this reason alone, I would say this is a significant book.

2. The Book of Jonah teaches that *salvation is not by works*, but by faith which leads to repentance. This little book is read by orthodox Jews on the great Day of Atonement, Yom Kippur. The way to God is not by works of righteousness which we have done, but by the blood of a substitutionary sacrifice provided by the Lord. The most significant statement in the Book of Jonah is in the second chapter. "Salvation is of the LORD" (Jonah 2:9). He is the author of salvation; He erected the great building of our salvation; He is the architect.

3. The third great purpose of this book is to show that *God's purpose of grace cannot be frustrated.* Jonah refused to go to Nineveh, but God was still going to get the message to Nineveh. The interesting thing in this particular case is that Jonah was going to be the witness for God in Nineveh—he didn't know he was going there, but he did go.

4. The fourth great truth in this book is that *God will not cast us aside for faithlessness.* He may not use you, but He will not cast you aside. There are a lot of football players sitting on the bench; in fact, more sit on the bench than play in the game. A player is called out to play only when it is believed that he can make a contribution to the game. If you and I are faithless, God may bench us; but we are still wearing our uniform, and He will not cast us aside. Anytime we want to get back in the game of life and do His will, He will permit us to do it.

5. The fifth great truth is that *God is good and gracious.* Read Jo-

nah 4:2 for the most penetrating picture of God in the entire Bible. It is wrong to say that the Old Testament reveals a God of wrath and the New Testament reveals a God of love. He is no vengeful deity in the Book of Jonah.

6. The sixth and last great teaching is that *God is the God of Gentiles*. When God chose Abraham, in effect He said to the Gentiles, "I'm going to have to leave you for awhile because of the sin that has come into the human family. I'm going to prepare salvation for you through a man and a nation, and I'll bring the Redeemer, the Savior, into the world through them." Now God has a salvation for all mankind. I have written Romans 3:29 over the Book of Jonah in my Bible. Paul writes, "Is he the God of the Jews only? is he not also of the Gentiles? Yes, of the Gentiles also." The Book of Jonah reveals that even in the Old Testament God did not forget the Gentiles. If He was willing to save a woman like Rahab the harlot, and a brutal, cruel nation like the Assyrians, including inhabitants of Nineveh, its capital, then I want to say to you that God is in the business of saving sinners.

OUTLINE

There are two approaches to the study of the Book of Jonah. The one that is the most popular and is followed by most commentators is to note the striking resemblance between Jonah and Paul. Both Paul and Jonah were missionaries to the Gentiles, both were cast into the sea, both were witnesses to the sailors on board the boat, and both were used to deliver those sailors from death. There are other striking comparisons, which a careful study would reveal. Including his trip to Rome, which I consider to be a missionary journey, there were actually four missionary journeys of the apostle Paul. The four chapters of the Book of Jonah may be divided into four missionary journeys of Jonah. The first journey was into the fish; the second was to the dry land; the third was to Nineveh; and the fourth brought him to the heart of God.

That is a very good and reliable division of this little book, but it never actually satisfied me, and I have attempted to make an outline of the book without making a comparison with Paul. Very frankly, I had more difficulty outlining the little Book of Jonah than I did the Book of Revelation.

I have another approach to outlining Jonah, and I want to tell you how it came about. Many years ago, I was waiting for the train one night in Nashville, Tennessee. I was returning to seminary, and at that time I was working on outlines for each book of the Bible, for I started early in that type of ministry. But I couldn't figure out an outline for Jonah. When I got to the Union Station in Nashville, I discovered that the train was late and that I would have to wait thirty minutes to an hour. I did what I'm sure you do whenever you must wait in an airport or railroad station. I walked around for quite awhile before I sat down. I walked by the popcorn machine; I walked by the cigar stand (today they call them gift shops); I walked by the soda pop vendor; and I walked by the restaurant that was there. I just kept walking around, and I came to the railroad timetable. As I was looking at the timetable, it occurred to me that the Book of Jonah could be outlined according to a timetable.

Three important things are to be found on a timetable. The first is the time and place that the train or plane is leaving. Second, there is the destination of the train or plane. Finally, you need to know the time it will arrive at its destination. I go to many places today on speaking engagements, and if I fly, there are three things that are important to know: the time I leave, my destination, and the time of my arrival.

Therefore, if we look at the Book of Jonah as a timetable, this becomes my outline for the book:

	LEAVE	DESTINATION	ARRIVE
Chapter 1	Israel	Nineveh	Fish
	(Samaria or Gath-hepher)		
Chapter 2	Fish	Nineveh	Dry Land
Chapter 3	Dry Land	Nineveh	Nineveh
Chapter 4	Nineveh	Gourd Vine	Heart of God

CHAPTER 1

THEME: Call and commission of Jonah; Jonah goes west; the great wind; Jonah arrives in the fish

CALL AND COMMISSION OF JONAH

Now the word of the LORD came unto Jonah the son of Amittai saying, [Jonah 1:1].

Jonah is identified for us as a prophet and as the son of Amittai. (See the Introduction for a detailed discussion of the evidence that Jonah was a historical character.)

Arise, go to Nineveh, that great city, and cry against it; for their wickedness is come up before me [Jonah 1:2].

This is God's call and commission of Jonah to go to Nineveh. The city of Nineveh is called "that great city." It was the capital of the Assyrian Empire and was located on the Tigris River. It was *the* world power in that day. Later on, we will deal with the matter of the size of the city, because it is emphasized two more times in this book. Here the emphasis is actually upon the wickedness of the city. It is a great city but great in wickedness. Its wickedness is so great that it has come up before God, and He has now determined that He will judge the city—that is, if the city does not turn to Him.

JONAH GOES WEST

But Jonah rose up to flee unto Tarshish from the presence of the LORD, and went down to Joppa; and he found a ship going to Tarshish: so he paid the fare thereof, and went down into it, to go with them unto Tarshish from the presence of the LORD [Jonah 1:3].

Jonah leaves his hometown of Gath-hepher in the northern kingdom of Israel and, with this call and commission from God, you would think that he plans to head for the city of Nineveh. Jonah would have had to go *east* from Israel to get to Nineveh. Instead of going in that direction, he does a very strange thing. He goes down to Joppa and buys a ticket on the first boat for Tarshish. Tarshish was a city founded by the Phoenicians on the southern coast of Spain. It was the jumping-off place of the *west*.

What we have before us is a greater problem that the problem of Jonah in the fish. The problem in the Book of Jonah is not the fish—it's Jonah. God asks him to go to Nineveh, but he buys a ticket for Tarshish. God tells him to go east—Jonah decides not to obey God, and he goes west. The question naturally arises: Why did Jonah do this? There are several reasons:

1. Jonah hated the Ninevites, and he did not want them saved. There was a basis for his hatred. Assyria was one of the most brutal nations of the ancient world. They were feared and dreaded by all the peoples of that day. They used very cruel methods of torture and could extract information from their captives very easily. One of the procedures was to take a man out onto the sands of the desert and bury him up to his neck—nothing but his head would stick out. Then they would put a thong through his tongue and leave him there to die as the hot, penetrating sun would beat down upon his head. It is said that a man would go mad before he died. That was one of the "nice little things" the Assyrians hatched up.

As an army, the Assyrians moved in an unusual manner. One of the reasons the Babylonians were able to overcome them was the slowness of the march of the Assyrian army. They took their families with them and had very little order in the army. They moved as a mob across the countryside. It is very easy to see that their disorder would militate against them. However, when they moved down like a plague of locusts upon a town or village, it is said that they were so feared and dreaded that on some occasions an entire town would commit suicide rather than fall into the hands of the brutal Assyrians. You can see that they were not loved by the peoples round about.

We also know that at this time the Assyrians were making forays into the northern kingdom of Israel. For a long time, it was Syria and the northern kingdom that fought against each other, but they finally came to an alliance because of the threat of Assyria to the north and east of them. However, Assyria eventually took both Syria and Israel into captivity. When the Assyrians were beginning to penetrate into a nation they hoped to conquer, they would make a surprise attack upon a city, take captive the women, and then brutally slay the men and the children. We don't know this for sure, but it is reasonable to conceive that the Assyrians had come down against Jonah's hometown of Gath-hepher at one time. They may have come even to his home, and he may have seen his own father and mother cruelly, brutally slain before his eyes. Or he might have seen his sisters raped by the Assyrians. At least we know that Jonah hated the Assyrians, and he did not want them saved. Therefore, he goes in the opposite direction—he's not going to carry God's message to them.

2. There is a second reason that Jonah went west. Somebody might point out that Jonah's message was one of salvation. His message was to be one of judgment. Although it is true that it was to be a message of judgment, Jonah knew God, and it was because Jonah knew God that he went in the opposite direction. He knew that if he went to Nineveh with a message of judgment and if the people of the city turned to God in repentance, God would not judge them but would save the city! Jonah didn't want that city saved. It just wasn't something he looked forward to. And so he went in the opposite direction.

3. A third reason that Jonah went in the opposite direction was because he was a disobedient prophet of God—there is no question about that. He was out of the will of God, very much like the prodigal son. The prodigal son ran away from home. He didn't want to live under the will of his father, and so he went to the far country. Jonah was out of the will of God. He was a prophet who is certainly not in step with God. We will find that the entire fourth chapter deals with his rebellion and how God brought him back into step with Himself.

4. Here is a fourth and final reason that Jonah disobeyed God. Have you ever noticed that in the Old Testament God never sent His

messengers as missionaries to other countries? The method that God used in the Old Testament was really the opposite of His method today. Israel was to serve and worship God as a nation that was located at the crossroads of the world, where the three continents of Europe, Asia, and Africa meet. The nations of that day, if they were not traveling by water, would take the route through the land of Israel. God took the people of Israel, put them there at the crossroads, and had them build a temple to worship Him in order that they might witness to God by serving Him. Their witness was to a world that was looking in on them. The invitation was, "Come, and let us go up to the house of the Lord and worship Him." Israel witnessed by serving God at the crossroads of the world, and the world came to them.

For example, the Queen of Sheba came from the ends of the earth to Israel. Why did she come? She had heard how they worshiped and, when she got there, she found that there was an altar there for sinners. That was the thing which brought her to a saving knowledge of God. If you read the historical record, you will find that not only did she come but also the kings of the earth came to hear the wisdom of Solomon. During that brief period, Israel did witness to the world; they witnessed not by going out as missionaries but by the world coming in to them.

We are given only the one example of the Queen of Sheba in the Old Testament. In the New Testament we have the examples of one son of Ham, one son of Japheth, and one son of Shem who were converted—the Ethiopian eunuch, Saul of Tarsus, and Cornelius, the Roman centurion. Although we are given only these examples, there were literally thousands and, later, millions who were led to Christ.

However, for the church today the method is the opposite of that in the Old Testament. I think it was rather startling for the twelve disciples, all of whom were Israelites brought up on the Old Testament, when the Lord Jesus said to them, ". . . Go ye into all the world, and preach the gospel . . ." (Mark 16:15). I imagine they looked at each other and said, "My, this is something brand new! We did not know that it was to be done this way." Instead of, "Come up to Jerusalem," the Lord Jesus said, "Beginning at Jerusalem, you are to go now to Judea, Samaria, and on to the ends of the earth" (see Acts 1:8). That is the method today. We often criticize Israel for their failure, but we build a church on the corner and expect the world to come to us, when instead we are supposed to be going out to the world. It took me years to learn that, but that is why the burden of my ministry today is to get the Word of God out to the world via radio. We believe that this is God's method today.

But that wasn't the method in Jonah's day, and Jonah was surprised when God said to him, "Arise, go to Nineveh." I think Jonah was the same kind of man as Simon Peter, and he probably talked back to the Lord. I think he said, "Wait a minute here! You never sent Elijah down to Egypt, and You never sent Elisha over into India. Why are You asking me to do something You've never asked a prophet to do before?" I have great sympathy for Jonah. He didn't understand why God would want to change His method. However, this book reveals that God is the God of the Gentiles. Paul wrote in Romans 3:29, "Is he the God of the Jews only? is he not also of the Gentiles? Yes, of the Gentiles also." Jonah could say amen to that statement but not at this point in time. It wasn't until after the experiences related in this book that he realized that God is the God of the Gentiles also.

"And he found a ship going to Tarshish: so he paid the fare thereof, and went down into it, to go with them unto Tarshish from the presence of the LORD." Jonah's experience may be helpful to you if you are having a difficult time and wonder if you are in the will of God. Although I cannot tell you whether or not you are in God's will, I can say this to you: The fact that you are having a difficult time is not a proof that you are out of the will of God. Rather, it may be a proof that you are in the will of God. If you are having it too easy today and things are breaking just right for you in every direction, and if that is all you are using to interpret that you are in the will of God, then you are leaning on a poor, broken reed, and it will not hold you up in time of a crisis.

Let's look closely at the illustration of Jonah. Here is a man who hears God's call and heads in the opposite direction. He is definitely out of the will of God. He goes down to Joppa, and when he goes down there, he encounters no problems. He finds a ship. He buys a ticket. He gets on board the ship, and he goes to sleep! Everything is lovely.

I'm of the opinion that Jonah could give a testimony, the kind of which I have often heard. Jonah went down to buy the ticket, perhaps wondering if he were in God's will or not. (He should have known he wasn't. But a lot of us say that we wonder whether we are or not.) He was standing in line to buy a ticket, and the ticket agent said to the man right ahead of Jonah, "I'm sorry, but all space is sold." Jonah was about to turn away when the phone rang and the ticket agent answered it. A Mr. Goldberg was calling to say that he was in the hospital, having suddenly taken sick, and he would not be able to make the trip. So Jonah waited, and the ticket agent turned to him and said, "Brother, are you lucky! I've just had a cancellation." Jonah must have thought, *I sure feel lucky. I feel more than that—maybe this means I'm in God's will.*

How many Christians think like that today? If they are having a difficult time, they say, "Oh, I am out of the will of God." If things are going easy and everything works out well, they say, "Oh, I must be in the will of God." My friend, I am of the opinion that if you are having problems, it may be that the Devil is getting a little uneasy because you are growing and proving effective for God. I have found this to be true in my own ministry. Just because you are having trouble does not mean you are out of the will of God.

Everything seemed to be propitious for a very pleasant journey for Jonah. Everything had worked out so well. Someone has called this "the fortuitous occurrence of circumstances." But we know that Jonah is going in the wrong direction and that God will have to put him inside a fish in order to turn him around.

God's men down through the centuries, both in the Bible and out of the Bible, have not found the going so easy. It hasn't always been so propitious. Things have been difficult. I have thrilled at the story of David Livingstone, but that man really suffered. If I had been penetrating dark Africa as he did, after a few of the rough experiences that he had, it would have been very easy to say in a very pious voice, "I think it is the will of God for us to turn around and go home." Likewise, John G. Patton, a missionary in the New Hebrides, met disappointment on every hand. He had to overcome handicaps daily, but this is the way God leads.

We read in the Book of Hebrews, "And others had trial of cruel mockings and scourgings, yea, moreover of bonds and imprisonment: they were stoned, they were sawn asunder, were tempted, were slain with the sword: they wandered about in sheepskins and goatskins; being destitute, afflicted, tormented; (of whom the world was not worthy:) they wandered in deserts, and in mountains, and in dens and caves of the earth" (Heb. 11:36–38). We read also in Hebrews that some *escaped* the edge of the sword by faith, but others by faith were *slain* by the sword. Therefore, you cannot always interpret the good circumstances as being God's will and the unfavorable circumstances as not being God's will.

Jonah is on shipboard now; and, as the ship pulls out, I imagine that Jonah stands on the top deck, smiling as the land fades away in the distance. He may be saying to himself, "My, what a beautiful journey this is going to be!" But we will find that this man is not going to have it quite that easy.

THE GREAT WIND

But the Lord sent out a great wind into the sea, and there was a mighty tempest in the sea, so that the ship was like to be broken [Jonah 1:4].

"But the Lord sent out a great wind into the sea." God was responsible for this storm. I call your attention to that at the very beginning. This storm is supernatural.

The storm on the Sea of Galilee, during which our Lord was asleep in the boat, was such that those men on board knew that they were going to perish. They were experienced with that sea and knew that it was a storm which they could not weather and that their boat soon would be at the bottom of the sea. It was a supernatural storm also, but Satan was responsible for that one in an attempt to destroy the Lord Jesus. Peter came to Him and said, ". . . carest thou not that we perish?" (Mark 4:38)—for that is what would have happened had He not intervened.

Here in the Book of Jonah, God is using a storm, and He is using it for a good purpose. He is going to save a city with this storm. He is going to turn around a prophet who has been going the wrong way and start him going the right way.

> **Then the mariners were afraid, and cried every man unto his god, and cast forth the wares that were in the ship into the sea, to lighten it of them. But Jonah was gone down into the sides of the ship; and he lay, and was fast asleep [Jonah 1:5].**

These "mariners" are sailors accustomed to the Mediterranean, and they detect that this is no *natural* storm.

"But Jonah was gone down into the sides of the ship; and he lay, and was fast asleep." I once entertained the popular viewpoint that if a man gets out of the will of God and into sin, he will be tormented with a bad conscience and will simply be in misery. Is that true of Jonah? Jonah is definitely out of the will of God, going the opposite way, actually running away from the presence of God. He wants to get as far from Nineveh as he possibly can, and he is headed for Tarshish. Yet he is confident that everything is all right. He can sleep in this storm when even the sailors are frightened, and these sailors are a bunch of pagans, worshiping all kinds of gods.

> **So the shipmaster came to him, and said unto him, What meanest thou, O sleeper? arise, call upon thy God, if so be that God will think upon us, that we perish not [Jonah 1:6].**

In effect, the shipmaster says, "You sleepy-head, you! Do you mean that you can sleep in a storm like this?" Jonah could. In fact, he is the only one on board who could sleep! The shipmaster goes on, "Arise, call upon thy God, if so be that God will think upon us, that we perish not." So Jonah now comes up on deck, and he sees this great storm they are in which is threatening to send the ship to the bottom.

> **And they said every one to his fellow, Come, and let us cast lots, that we may know for whose cause this evil is**

upon us. So they cast lots, and the lot fell upon Jonah [Jonah 1:7].

On other occasions when I have taught the Book of Jonah, some folk have misunderstood me at this point and have thought that I approved of gambling. I hope you will follow me very carefully at this time. I think that gambling is an awful curse. I believe that the use of the lottery and of gambling in order to raise revenue for the government will ultimately corrupt our people and our nation. In the end it will be more destructive than it could possibly be helpful.

Other folk are quick to point out that this was a superstitious thing the sailors were doing, casting lots to see why this evil had come upon them. They cast lots, and it fell on Jonah. Apparently God was in this and used this, but that does not mean that God approved of it.

These sailors cast lots. Can God use something like that? I want to share with you an experience that I had in my first pastorate. The very wonderful pastor whom I followed there told me about a certain family in the church. The wife and the little girl, a beautiful, redheaded little girl, were both believers and attended the church, but the pastor had not been able to reach the father, the head of the home. At Christmastime that year, the father came to church. I whispered to several people to be friendly to him, and they all shook hands with him and greeted him. His criticism was that we overdid it! We were too friendly. So at Eastertime when he again came to church, I simply told the folk that he didn't want us to shake hands with him and be friendly. So they didn't, and I just barely shook his hand at the door. His criticism of the church then was that we were too cold. Now there was a fellow you couldn't please at all! When I went to visit him, he practically ordered me out of the house—he didn't want me to talk to him about the Lord.

About six months later, as I was getting ready for bed one night—in fact, I already had on my pajamas—the doorbell rang. I opened the door, and there stood this man with a very frightened look on his face. I let him in, and we sat down to talk. He told me that he ran a dry cleaning place and had a woman working there for him at the desk as a cashier. One morning she had come to work and told him, "I went to a fortune-teller last night, and the fortune-teller told me that I'm going to die suddenly." Both he and the woman had laughed about it. Then she went on to say, "The fortune-teller also said that the man I am working for is going to die suddenly." They laughed again because they thought it was all preposterous and ridiculous.

But about two days later, as she stepped off the streetcar, that woman was hit by a car and was killed almost instantly. I want to tell you, when he heard it, he really became frightened. It was the very night when he came and knocked on my door. He said to me, "I must be next."

I told him, "Well, I think I can relieve your fear there. The fortune-teller had nothing in the world to do with her death—she had no prior knowledge of it. This is just one of those strange circumstances of life which we call a coincidence. This doesn't mean that you will die."

He said, "But I want to be prepared. Would you explain to me the plan of salvation?" I got down on the floor in my pajamas, with some wrapping paper and a piece of crayon, and I outlined the plan of salvation for him. I explained to him how God had sent Christ into the world to die for our sins. That man was ready that night, and he accepted Christ as his Savior.

I have always thought that the Devil had pushed that fellow a little too far, because he was responsible for the man getting saved. Very frankly, God can use things like that. He says that He will make the wrath of man to praise Him, and He can also make the superstition of man to praise Him.

Those sailors on board with Jonah were superstitious fellows. God used their superstition. They cast lots, and the lot fell upon Jonah. Notice what happens—

> **Then said they unto him, Tell us, we pray thee, for whose cause this evil is upon us; What is thine occupation? and whence comest thou? what is thy country? and of what people art thou? [Jonah 1:8].**

Jonah apparently has had some time to talk to these sailors, but he hasn't told them much about himself. He certainly is no witness for

God. A man out of the will of God can never be an effective witness for God. That is something very important for us to keep in mind.

Notice what Jonah did not tell them. First of all they say to him, "We want to ask you some questions since this evil has fallen on us. What is thine occupation?" Jonah hasn't told anybody he is a prophet; he's kept quiet on that. "And whence comest thou?" Jonah hasn't told them he is from Gath-hepher in the northern kingdom of Israel. He hasn't said anything about his hometown. "What is thy country?" He hasn't said that he is a citizen of Israel. "And of what people art thou?" He hasn't said that he belongs to the Israelite people who have a revelation of the living and true God. He hasn't explained that he is a prophet who represents the living God and who has been called to go to Nineveh to bring a message of hope and salvation. Jonah hasn't said any of that. Why? He is entirely out of the will of God.

> **And he said unto them, I am an Hebrew; and I fear the LORD, the God of heaven, which hath made the sea and the dry land [Jonah 1:9].**

"I am an Hebrew"—that meant a lot. The Hebrews were known to be monotheistic; that is, they worshiped one God, never an idol. They had no other gods before them but worshiped the God who is the Creator. Jonah says, "I fear the LORD, the God of heaven, which hath made the sea and the dry land." Jonah tells them that he worships the God who made the ocean which they could see right before them being so stirred up by the storm. He made the sea, and He made the dry land also. I think these sailors knew about Israel, but they were pagan and had no knowledge of the living and true God.

> **Then were the men exceedingly afraid, and said unto him, Why hast thou done this? For the men knew that he fled from the presence of the LORD, because he had told them [Jonah 1:10].**

Although he could sleep with it very nicely, without question Jonah had a bad conscience. Jonah tells the sailors, "The reason I am taking

this trip is for a pleasure trip. Actually, I had business over in
Nineveh, but I decided not to go over there. I know that I am getting
away from my God in making this trip." But Jonah hasn't divulged too
much information to them.

These men say to Jonah, "Why hast thou done this?" May I say to
you, that is the good question that the unbeliever sometimes asks of
the believer—and can be an embarrassing one.

When I was a pastor of a church in Los Angeles, an unsaved man
who had visited the church came to see me. I had met him before in a
business in downtown Los Angeles and had invited him to come to
church. He said to me, "Is So-and-so a member of your church?" I
said, "Yes, and he's an officer in the church." He said, "I've known
that man for several years, and I've done business with him. I never
would have dreamed that he is a Christian. If I were a Christian, I
would not do the things that man does." You know, it's embarrassing
when an unbeliever says to a Christian, "Why are you doing this? I
thought you were a child of God." I think Jonah must have turned
three or four different shades of red at this particular time.

JONAH ARRIVES IN THE FISH

**Then said they unto him, What shall we do unto thee,
that the sea may be calm unto us? for the sea wrought,
and was tempestuous [Jonah 1:11].**

These men recognize that they are up against a very hard decision,
and they want Jonah to make that decision. They ask him, "What shall
we do unto thee, that the sea may be calm unto us?" And Jonah gives
them a very straightforward answer—

**And he said unto them, Take me up, and cast me forth
into the sea; so shall the sea be calm unto you: for I
know that for my sake this great tempest is upon you
[Jonah 1:12].**

Jonah recognizes that the hand of God is in all of this and that God is moving in his life at this time. He knows that the only solution to the problem of the storm is to get him off the ship going to Tarshish. God has determined that this man is not going to Tarshish but to the place where He wants him to go.

> **Nevertheless the men rowed hard to bring it to the land; but they could not: for the sea wrought, and was tempestuous against them [Jonah 1:13].**

These pagan sailors certainly stand in a good light at this point. Although they are pagan and heathen, they do not want to throw him overboard. They try their best to get the ship out of the storm. They row as hard as they can to bring the ship to land, but they cannot do it. At this particular point in the book, these pagan sailors stand in a better light than Jonah does and prove to be rather outstanding men.

> **Wherefore they cried unto the LORD, and said, We beseech thee, O LORD, we beseech thee, let us not perish for this man's life, and lay not upon us innocent blood: for thou, O LORD, hast done as it pleased thee [Jonah 1:14].**

Notice the change that is taking place in these men's lives. They are turning now to the living and true God. Of course, they are turning in their desperation. They call upon God to forgive them for what they are going to do, because they have no other alternative.

> **So they took up Jonah, and cast him forth into the sea: and the sea ceased from her raging [Jonah 1:15].**

This reveals very definitely that it was a supernatural storm under God's control.

> **The the men feared the LORD exceedingly, and offered a sacrifice unto the LORD, and made vows [Jonah 1:16].**

The fear of the Lord, we are told in Scripture, is the beginning of wisdom. "Then the men feared the LORD exceedingly." Did they fear their god? No. They feared the one who is the Creator of the sea and of the land.

"And offered a sacrifice unto the LORD." That sacrifice points to Jesus Christ—there is no alternative.

"And made vows." What vows do these men make? They vow to the Lord that they will now serve Him. Through this experience, they now turn to the living and true God. So something good is accomplished by the storm, by Jonah's being on board the ship, and by his being cast overboard.

Notice now what happens to Jonah—

Now the LORD had prepared a great fish to swallow up Jonah. And Jonah was in the belly of the fish three days and three nights [Jonah 1:17].

The Greek word translated as "whale" in Matthew 12:40 is *kêtos*, meaning "a huge fish." It is called here "a great fish." I do not think it was a whale, but the thing that is important is the fact that the fish was prepared by the Lord for this special event. I am of the opinion that we have a miracle in this fish in the sense that it was a specially prepared fish to swallow up Jonah.

"And Jonah was in the belly of the fish three days and three nights." Notice that it does not say that Jonah was alive inside the fish.

A review of my timetable for the Book of Jonah shows that in chapter 1 Jonah leaves Israel, his destination is Nineveh, but he arrives in the fish.

CHAPTER 2

THEME: When did Jonah pray? Jonah's prayer; Jonah arrives on the dry land

Our timetable for chapter 2 tells us that Jonah is going to leave the fish, his destination is still Nineveh, and he will arrive on the dry land. First, however, we want to examine the experience of this man inside the fish.

WHY DID JONAH PRAY?

Then Jonah prayed unto the LORD his God out of the fish's belly [Jonah 2:1].

Immediately someone is going to say to me, "You believe that Jonah was dead inside the fish and that God raised him from the dead, but it says here that Jonah prayed unto the Lord God out of the fish's belly—that means he was alive inside the fish." That is true, but my question is: When did Jonah pray this prayer? Did he pray this prayer when he first got into the fish? Or, when Jonah found himself inside the fish, did he say to himself, "My, I am really here in a precarious position, and things sure don't look good for me. I want to prepare a prayer to send to God that He'll hear and answer"? Did he decide to write out his prayer, work on it for a couple of days, memorize it, and then on the third day say the prayer to God? If Jonah did that, then my interpretation of this is all wrong—I'm all wet, if you please. But if I know human nature at all, Jonah didn't wait very long to pray this prayer. When he found himself in this condition, you can be sure of one thing: he *immediately* went to prayer before God. In fact, I think he prayed on the way down, and by the time he got into the fish's tummy, it was time to say amen.

Men don't pray a prepared prayer in time of crisis. They get down to business immediately when the crisis comes. I am reminded of a friend of mine in the ministry who lost the index finger on his right hand below the first joint—there was nothing left but a stub. When anyone would ask him how he was called to the ministry, he would hold up that little stub of a finger and wiggle it, and then he would tell his story.

When he was a boy, an evangelist came to their church to hold meetings. The first night of the meetings, his dad, who was an officer in the church, made him sit on the front row, and the preacher really made that seat hot for him. He knew the preacher was talking right to him, although the preacher himself didn't realize it. His dad made him go to the meeting the second night, and he knew that if he went yet another time, he not only would accept Christ as his Savior but would also give his life to enter the ministry. He had a feeling even at that time that that would be his call. So that night after everybody went to bed, he got an extra shirt and his pajamas and ran off to Mississippi. There he got a job in a sawmill. I don't know if you are acquainted with the old-time sawmill. A man would take a great hook and would roll the logs over onto the carriage which would take the log on down to the big saw. The saw would then rip that log right down through the middle. My friend's job was to roll the logs onto the carriage.

One afternoon after he had worked there for about two weeks, he ran out of logs. So the foreman got some old logs which had not been run through the saw for one reason or another. There was one log among them that had already been ripped about halfway. For some reason they hadn't finished it but had pulled it back out. When my friend rolled that particular log over onto the carriage which carried it into the band saw, the place where the log had previously been ripped opened up, and the index finger on his right hand got caught in it. He felt himself being pulled along the carriage toward that big band saw. He began to yell at the top of his voice, but by that time, the other end of the log had hit the saw and was already going through. If you have ever been around a sawmill, you know that that makes a terrible racket—nobody could hear him. He was yelling at the top of his voice, very frightened as he found himself being pulled against his will right into that saw.

It would take only about forty-five seconds for him to get to the saw. His finger was way out in front of him, and the place where the log had been sawed was clamped down tight on it. His finger hit the saw and was cut off. But that released him, and he rolled to the side and was safe. In that forty-five seconds, he had prayed to the Lord. He accepted Christ as his Savior, promised the Lord he would go into the ministry and do His will, and told Him a lot of other things also! My preacher friend used to say that he told the Lord more in that forty-five seconds than he has ever told Him in an hour's prayer since then.

May I say to you, he prayed that prayer immediately when the crisis came. That's when I pray; that's when you pray. You don't *wait* to pray in a time of emergency. I recall one time on a plane when we got into unusually rough weather—I don't like flying even in good weather, and this rough weather was terrific. The minute the plane began to drop—it seemed to me like it was never going to quit dropping!—I began to pray. I didn't say, "I'm going to wait until we are off the plane, I'm going to wait until we get out of this storm before I pray." I began to pray right there and then. I'm sure that's what you do, and I'm almost sure that's what Jonah did, also.

So Jonah prayed this prayer as he went down from the mouth of the fish and through the esophagus. By the time, he went "kerplunk" into the fish's tummy, this man Jonah had already completed his prayer and had said amen. I think he prayed a great deal more than is recorded here—I think we have "the abridged edition" of it.

Some folk put a great deal of emphasis upon the time word *then*— "Then Jonah prayed unto the Lord his God out of the fish's belly." They assume that this means that after he had been in the fish three days and three nights, then he prayed. This is not what it means at all. It is characteristic of the Hebrew language to give the full account of something and then to go back and emphasize that which is important. This same technique is used in Genesis concerning the creation. We are given the six days of creation, and then God goes back and gives a detailed account of the creation of man, adding a great deal. To attempt to build an assumption on the little word *then* is very fallacious. It simply means that now Jonah is going to tell us the story in detail; he is going to tell us what really happened inside the fish.

JONAH'S PRAYER

**And said, I cried by reason of mine affliction unto the
LORD, and he heard me; out of the belly of hell cried I,
and thou heardest my voice [Jonah 2:2].**

"I cried by reason of mine affliction unto the LORD, and he heard me."
Notice first that God heard Jonah's prayer.

"Out of the belly of hell cried I." *The New Scofield Reference Bible*
translates this as "out of the belly of *sheol*," and that certainly is accurate for that is the original Hebrew word. *Sheol* is sometimes translated in Scripture by the word "grave" and in other places as "the
unseen world," meaning where the dead go. This is a word that, any
way you look at it, has to do with death. It is a word that always goes to
the cemetery, and you cannot take it anywhere else. Therefore, my
interpretation of what Jonah is saying is that the belly of the fish was
his grave, and a grave is a place for the dead—you do not put a live
man in a grave. Jonah recognized that he was going to die inside the
fish and that God would hear him and raise him from the dead.

Many years ago when I was still a young seminary student, I was
asked to preach for a brief period of time at the Westminster Presbyte-
rian Church in Atlanta, Georgia. I made the Sunday evening service
an evangelistic service. One night several young people came forward
when I gave the invitation. After the service I talked to them, and then
I went to the rear of the church. A young fellow was standing there,
and he told me, "I'm a student at Georgia Tech, and I would like to
accept Christ, but I have a hurdle, a problem that I can't overcome." I
asked him what his problem was, and he replied, "I just can't believe
that a man could live three days and three nights inside a fish."

I said, "Who told you that?"

"Well," he said, "I thought the Bible said so, and I know I've heard
preachers say so. And I've got a professor at school who spends his
time ridiculing that."

"My Bible doesn't say that Jonah was alive inside the fish," I told
him. Then I opened my Bible to the second chapter of Jonah and said,

"To begin with, this man Jonah makes it very clear that the belly of the fish was his grave. A grave is a place for the dead."

"Do you mean that he *died*? Then that means that God raised him from the dead!" the young man said. I told him he was exactly right—that is exactly what happened. He said, "That's a greater miracle than Jonah's being kept alive in the fish for three days." I agreed with him that it was a greater miracle because, as we shall see, we have records of other men who have lived through such experiences.

The important thing to note here is the Jonah cried unto the Lord out of the fish's belly, out of the belly of hell, out of the belly of *sheol*, out of the belly of the grave—and that is the place for the dead. Jonah felt like he was there to die and that he was in his grave. You must remember that he did not write this account while he was inside the fish but afterward.

I realize there are those who will not accept my viewpoint concerning this. When I wrote my first booklet on it, I felt very much alone. However, when the late Dr. M. R. DeHaan also took this viewpoint, many folk accepted it because of their confidence in him.

If you hold the other viewpoint that Jonah was alive, that's all right. God certainly could have kept Jonah alive. But, my friend, don't hold that viewpoint to the extent that you prevent a lot of young people from defending the Bible. This young man from Georgia Tech went back to college, and when his professor again brought up the subject of Jonah, he said to the professor, "Who told you that Jonah was alive inside the fish?" The professor said, "The Bible says so." This young fellow said to him, "Not my Bible." When they got out a Bible (which they had trouble finding) and looked at the Scripture, they found that it does not say that Jonah was alive inside the fish.

I want to share with you a letter that came to me from Austin, Texas, and which reveals the popular interpretation of the Book of Jonah:

Thank you for responding to my letter concerning Jonah. It is a mark of your dedication that you take time to answer such letters, since I am sure you get many. I believe you are doing a fine

work for the Lord, and in listening to you over the years, I think
you are not getting older but getting better.

(May I say to you, I'm getting older, but no one's kidding me, I'm not
getting better!) The letter continues:

Your story about your fear of flying and how you conquered it
brings meaning to a living faith, but as far as Jonah goes, you
are, I believe, putting in a private interpretation. You're straining the Word to make it say something it doesn't say. May I go
on to say that the fact that Jonah lived three days in the whale's
belly doesn't do any damage to the reference in Matthew
12:39-40.
   Why don't you take your Bible and read it again? If we forget the chapter designation, it helps. "And Jonah was in the
belly of the fish three days and three nights. Then Jonah prayed
unto the Lord his God out of the fish's belly." I guess that Jonah
did a lot of soul-searching during those three days. If you interpret this passage like you do, you must believe the writer
didn't have enough sense to put the story down in the sequence
it occurred.
   . . . You state that it assumed that Jonah was alive. Well, I
don't believe it is, but if you want to say that, I think your assumption [that he was dead] is the greater assumption, and I
hope you realize you are only assuming. My question to you is:
Why?

I appreciate that letter, and I recognize that the general and popular
interpretation is that Jonah was alive for three days and three nights
inside the fish, that he apparently had a very comfortable weekend
inside a "fish-tel" instead of a motel. I don't think he could have been
as comfortable as he would have been in a Holiday Inn, a Ramada Inn,
or a Hilton Hotel, but at least it is popularly believed that he spent
three days and three nights in there alive. In fact, when I was a boy in
Sunday school, I was given a little card on which Jonah was shown
inside the fish, sitting at a table! I don't know where that came from,

but that was the way he was pictured and, although I was just a little fellow, it rather disturbed me.

If you hold the viewpoint that Jonah was alive, you are with the majority today, even with the majority of the expositors of the Book of Jonah. You can feel comfortable in being with the majority, but of course, if you want to be *right*, you'll want to go along with me, I'm sure. I say this facetiously, of course.

However, I want to make this point very carefully and very seriously. It is not a question of whether God was *able* to keep Jonah alive inside the fish or not. God *could* keep him alive. The question is: *Did* God keep him alive? Was the miracle one of keeping him alive, or was the miracle in raising him from the dead? Since this book illustrates resurrection, I'm of the opinion that God raised him from the dead.

If, after I have had a little talk with Jonah in heaven, I learn that he was *alive* for three days and three nights inside that fish, then you can come by and say, "I told you so." Then I will have to confess that I was wrong. I am not, however, as the writer of this letter seems to think, taking an assumption and making a dogmatic statement.

I do want to say that I have had the privilege of teaching the Book of Jonah on quite a few college campuses, and I have found that the position I take does give ammunition to young people today. If you want to hold to the opposite viewpoint, don't get enraged and become irritated with my viewpoint, for you must recognize that it has been very helpful to a great many students. It has been the means, as in the case of the Georgia Tech student years ago, of bringing some to a saving knowledge of Christ.

It is also not a question of whether a man *can* live in a fish. Men have been swallowed by a fish or by a whale and have lived to tell the story. There have been recorded some remarkable stories. So that leads me to say that, if you believe Jonah was alive inside the fish, that is not too great a miracle because other men have had the same experience.

Many years ago here in Pasadena, California, there was a very excellent Bible teacher by the name of Miss Grace W. Kellogg. She gave me a copy of her little book, *The Bible Today*. She held the old viewpoint that Jonah was alive inside the fish, and she wanted me to see that Jonah could have been alive. Of course, I agree that he could have been alive, and if that is what Jonah means to have said, then I have really misunderstood him. Nonetheless, I would like to give you a quotation from Miss Kellogg's book which shows that it is possible for a man to be swallowed by a fish and live. There are many examples of it, and I am going to give you a few of those that she gave:

There are at least two known monsters of the deep who could easily have swallowed Jonah. They are the Balaenoptera Musculus or sulphur-bottom whale, and the Rhinodon Typicus or whale shark. Neither of these monsters of the deep have any teeth. They feed in an interesting way by opening their enormous mouths, submerging their lower jaw, and rushing through the water at terrific speed. After straining out the water, they swallow whatever is left. A sulphur-bottom whale, one hundred feet long, was captured off Cape Cod in 1933. His mouth was ten or twelve feet wide—so big he could easily have swallowed a horse. These whales have four to six compartments in their stomachs, in any one of which a colony of men could find free lodging. They might even have a choice of rooms, for in the head of this whale is a wonderful air storage chamber, an enlargement of the nasal sinus, often measuring seven feet high, seven feet wide, by fourteen feet long. If he has an unwelcome guest on board who gives him a headache, the whale swims to the nearest land and gets rid of the offender as he did Jonah.

The *Cleveland Plain Dealer* recently quoted an article by Dr. Ransome Harvey who said that a dog was lost overboard from a ship. It was found in the head of a whale six days later, alive and barking.

Frank Bullen, F.R.G.S., who wrote, "The Cruise of the Cachalot," tells of a shark fifteen feet in length which was found in the stomach of a whale. He says that when dying the whale ejects the contents of its stomach.

The late Dr. Dixon stated that in a museum in Beirut, Lebanon, there is a head of a whale shark big enough to swallow the largest man that history records! He also tells of a white shark of the Mediterranean which swallowed a whole horse; another swallowed a reindeer minus only its horns. In still another Mediterranean white shark was found a whole sea cow, about the size of an ox.

These facts show that Jonah could have been swallowed by either a whale or a shark. But has any other man besides Jonah been swallowed and lived to tell the tale? We know two such instances.

The famous French scientist, M. de Parville, writes of James Bartley, who in the region of the Falkland Islands near South America, was supposed to have been drowned at sea. Two days after his disappearance, the sailors made a catch of a whale. When it was cut up, much to their surprise they found their missing friend alive but unconscious inside the whale. He revived and has been enjoying the best of health ever since his adventure.

Dr. Harry Rimmer, President of the Research Science Bureau of Los Angeles, writes of another case. "In the *Literary Digest* we noticed an account of an English sailor who was swallowed by a gigantic Rhinodon in the English Channel. Briefly, the account stated that in the attempt to harpoon one of these monstrous sharks, this sailor fell overboard, and before he could be picked up again, the shark turned and engulfed him. Forty-eight hours after the accident occurred, the fish was sighted and slain. When the shark was opened by the sailors, they were amazed to find the man unconscious but alive! He was rushed to the hospital where he was found to be suffering from shock alone, and a few hours later was discharged as being physically fit. The account concluded by saying that the man was on exhibit in a London Museum at a shilling admittance fee; being advertised as 'The Jonah of the Twentieth Century.' "

In 1926 Dr. Rimmer met this man, and writes that his physical appearance was odd; his body was devoid of hair and patches of yellowish-brown color covered his entire skin.

If two men could exist for two days and nights inside of marine monsters, could not a prophet of God, under His direct care and protection, stand the experience a day and night longer—so why should we doubt God's Word?

This demonstrates the fact that a man *could* live in a fish, but it also takes away from the unusual character of Jonah's experience; that is, if these men lived and Jonah lived—and I am told there are even other records of such experiences—then what you have in the Book of Jonah is a record of something that is not really a great miracle. You simply have a record of an unusual incident that took place. I personally believe that the greater miracle is the fact that God raised him from the dead.

Again, I remind you that the question before us is not whether God could make a man live for three days, and three nights inside a fish; the question is: Did God do that? Is that what the record says?

For thou hadst cast me into the deep, in the midst of the seas; and the floods compassed me about: all thy billows and thy waves passed over me [Jonah 2:3].

We cannot treat this lightly. If Jonah lived in the fish, he also lived like a fish, because he was swamped by water. He says, "The floods compassed me about: all thy billows and thy waves passed over me." In other words, Jonah is saying, "I got wet." I think it is all wet to try to say that the man lived three days and three nights. I personally feel that the Devil gets us to argue about that, while we miss the great truth of the resurrection.

Then I said, I am cast out of thy sight; yet I will look again toward thy holy temple [Jonah 2:4].

"Then I said, I am cast out of thy sight"—Jonah is speaking of death. "Yet I will look again toward thy holy temple." Jonah believed that he would be raised from the dead. He had been brought up on the Old Testament, and I think that Jonah was one of the many in the northern kingdom who faithfully went down to Jerusalem to worship in the temple. The Israelites knew that Solomon's temple was the place to worship the living and true God. Jonah says, "I'm going to look again toward thy holy temple. God will raise me up again."

Does this sound to you like a man who is alive?—

The waters compassed me about, even to the soul: the depth closed me round about, the weeds were wrapped about my head [Jonah 2:5].

"The waters compassed me about, even to the soul." He's saying, "I got drenched. The depth closed me round about, the weeds were wrapped about my head." This sea monster had been eating a bunch of seaweeds. Some seaweeds that I have pulled out along the Pacific Coast are twenty-five feet long—and this monster had his tummy full of them! Jonah says, "I was down there, and I got these things all wrapped around my head." Do you think this man is describing a very pleasant weekend inside a fish? I don't think so—I think he is trying to tell us that he went down to the very depths and that he *died.*

I went down to the bottoms of the mountains; the earth with her bars was about me for ever: yet hast thou brought up my life from corruption, O LORD my God [Jonah 2:6].

"I went down to the bottoms of the mountains; the earth with her bars was about me for ever." This is a very interesting translation because it is in Elizabethan English; this is the way that death was spoken of. "The earth with her bars was about me for ever"—Jonah is speaking here of the bars of death, and that is the meaning of this translation.

"Yet hast thou brought up my life from corruption, O LORD my God." "Corruption" is death. The apostle Peter so used this word on the Day of Pentecost when he said that the Lord Jesus did not see corruption (see Acts 2:25–31). The miracle about the Lord Jesus is that when He died He *did not* see corruption—His body did not corrupt. That is the difference between Jonah's experience and our Lord's experience. Jonah *did* see corruption. His body apparently began to decay in those three days and three nights. "Yet hast thou brought up my life from corruption." What we have here, in my judgment, is a definite statement by Jonah that he *died*. The miracle here is resurrection, and that is a much greater miracle than for a man to live for three days inside a fish.

I think it is very important that we have a book in the Old Testament which teaches the resurrection of Jesus Christ. The Resurrection is one of the two pillars of our salvation upon which the ark of the church rests—the death of Christ and the resurrection of Christ. They are both taught in the Old Testament, and this book illustrates His resurrection.

When my soul fainted within me I remembered the LORD: and my prayer came in unto thee, into thine holy temple [Jonah 2:7].

I think a normal explanation of this would be that when this man was swallowed by the fish, he was frightened. He began immediately to call out to God to deliver him as he found himself going down the esophagus of that fish.

"My soul fainted within me." It must have been at least five minutes before Jonah lapsed into unconsciousness, but before he did, he said, "I remembered the LORD." *This* is when he prayed his prayer. Don't try to tell me that he prayed his prayer on the third day, after he'd spent three days in their under conviction and soul-searching! Jonah has said that his soul got wet, and now he says that his soul fainted with him—that means he lost consciousness inside the fish.

"And my prayer came in unto thee, into thine holy temple." Before he lapsed into unconsciousness and before death came to him, this man had already prayed his prayer.

Jonah now makes an observation here, and it is one of the many maxims that you find in the Word of God—

They that observe lying vanities forsake their own mercy [Jonah 2:8].

I have tried to arrive at a satisfactory explanation of this verse, and so far I have been unable to do so. However, I will have to give you the explanation I have: This is another of the great principles in Scripture. Vanity is emptiness. Jonah is speaking here of those who observe that which is empty, that which is vain, that which is just a dream and is not going to come to pass. Jonah calls it a *lying emptiness*. He says that they forsake the only mercy they can receive. Jonah says at this time, "I called out to the living and true God. I no longer was playing the pouting prophet, rushing off to Tarshish in the opposite direction because I hated the Ninevites and didn't want them saved. *Now* I am dealing with reality. I'm getting right down to the nitty-gritty." (And, my friend, there was a whole lot of nitty-gritty inside that fish!) This man says, "I'm getting right down to business with God. I appealed to Him, to His mercy, and I found that He was merciful to me."

Jonah cried out to God, and now he shows his gratitude by saying this:

> **But I will sacrifice unto thee with the voice of thanksgiving; I will pay that that I have vowed. Salvation is of the LORD [Jonah 2:9].**

"But I will sacrifice unto thee with the voice of thanksgiving." Friend, I don't suppose you and I can possibly conceive of the thanksgiving that was in this man's heart and life when the fish vomited him out onto the dry land. He was a mess at that time, but he lifted his voice in thanksgiving to God for having delivered him and raised him from the dead.

"I will pay that that I have vowed." Do you know what Jonah's vow was? Can't you imagine what it was? I believe that he now says to the Lord, "I'll go to Nineveh." Before he had said, "I won't go to Nineveh." But he's changed his mind—God has changed it for him—and now he makes a vow that he will go to Nineveh.

The Lord has to deal with many of us like that. He has never put me through a fish, but He did give me cancer. Don't misunderstand me, I'm not blaming Him for that—He was judging me. He has also chastised me since then, because I thought that I had learned all the lessons an old man ought to learn, but I found out that I hadn't learned them. I am prepared to say the same thing Jonah said. I am thankful to Him for the trials He has permitted to come to me and for His deliverance from them. I've made vows to God; I've promised Him that I would devote the rest of my life to giving out His Word—that is what He has called me to do. Many people find fault and do not like the way I do it—I'm not entirely satisfied myself; I wish I could do it better—but I've made a vow to God, and I understand the vow this man Jonah made. He said, "I'm going to Nineveh, Lord, and I'm going to do what You want me to do."

"Salvation is of the LORD." In my judgment this is the most important statement that we find in the Book of Jonah. I think it is very, very important. Notice what he says: "I will pay that that I have vowed. Salvation is of the LORD"—he is speaking of deliverance.

There are several things about this that we need to note. Salvation is *God's work for us*. Salvation is *never man's work for God*. God cannot save us by our works, because the only thing that we can present to Him is imperfection, and God simply does not accept imperfection. However, we are unable to present perfection to Him. If it depended on us or our works, if it depended on our *doing* something, we could never be saved. To begin with, we are lost sinners, dead in trespasses and sins. If deliverance is to come, it will have to come to us like it did to Jonah, who was dead and hopeless in that fish. If he is to live, if he is to be used of God (and he is going to be used), it will be because "Salvation is of the LORD." And if you ever get saved, it is because salvation is of the Lord.

Salvation is such a wonderful thing that you can put it into three tenses: I *have been* saved—past tense; I *am being* saved—present tense; I *shall be* saved—future tense. So salvation is God's work from beginning to end. Let's look for a moment at what Scripture has to say about this.

1. *I have been saved*—past tense. The Lord Jesus Christ said, "Verily, verily, I say unto you, He that heareth my word, and believeth on him that sent me, hath everlasting life . . ." (John 5:24). The moment you trust Christ you *have* everlasting life. That is something that took place in the past for those who are Christians today. If sometime in the past you trusted Christ, that was all His work—you trusted what He

did. "He that believeth on the Son hath everlasting life . . ." (John 3:36). You received life when you trusted Christ. You did nothing, nothing whatsoever—He offered it to you as a gift. ". . . the gift of God is eternal life through Jesus Christ our Lord" (Rom. 6:23). I have been saved. How was I saved? By trusting Christ and His work. It was "Not by works of righteousness which we have done, but according to his mercy he saved us, by the washing of regeneration, and renewing of the Holy Ghost" (Titus 3:5).

2. *I am being saved*—present tense. God is not through with us; He intends to continue to work in our lives. We are told ". . . work out your own salvation with fear and trembling. For it is God which worketh in you both to will and to do of his good pleasure" (Phil. 2:12–13). You can't work it out until God has worked it in. Paul could say, "For by grace are ye saved through faith; and that not of yourselves: it is the gift of God: not of works, lest any man should boast" (Eph. 2:8–9). That's great, but the apostle didn't stop there; he went on to say, "For we are his workmanship . . ." (Eph. 2:10). His workmanship? Yes. "Created in Christ Jesus"—we were given a new life; Paul adds, "Created in Christ Jesus *unto good works*." So that now by the power of the Holy Spirit, the child of God is to produce fruit. The Lord Jesus said that He wanted us to bring forth much fruit (see John 15:1–5). Paul writes in Galatians, "But the fruit of the Spirit is love, joy, peace, longsuffering, gentleness, goodness, faith, meekness, temperance: against such there is no law" (Gal. 5:22–23). All of these marvelous, wonderful graces are His work, and He wants to work them in you today.

You and I ought to be growing in grace and in the knowledge of Christ. I am being saved—I ought to be a better Christian today than I was last year. I get a little discouraged in that connection, because sometimes I feel that I'm like the proverbial cat which climbed up three feet on the pole in the daytime but slipped back five feet at night! I feel like I haven't gotten very far, but nevertheless, there has been some growth. Don't be satisfied with me, because He is not through with me yet. "Salvation is of the LORD."

3. *I will be saved*—future tense. There is coming a day when I will

be saved. Paul said to that young preacher, Timothy, "All scripture is given by inspiration of God, and is profitable for doctrine, for reproof, for correction, for instruction in righteousness" (2 Tim. 3:16). As Paul talked to him about the wonderful Word of God, he also said, ". . . from a child thou hast known the holy scriptures, which are able to make thee wise unto salvation . . ." (2 Tim. 3:15). Since Timothy was already saved, what did Paul mean when he said, "which are able to make thee wise unto salvation"? He meant that the Scriptures would enable Timothy to grow and enable him to live for God.

But even when we come to the end of life, we are not complete. Dwight L. Moody, the great evangelist, used to tell about the time when he heard Henry Varley, then an unknown preacher. As Moody sat in the balcony, he heard Varley say, "The world has yet to see what God can do with a man who is fully yielded to Him." Dwight L. Moody, just a young fellow at that time, said to himself, "By the grace of God, I will be that man." But when he was dying, Moody said, "I wanted to be that man, but it is still true that the world has yet to see what God can do with a man who is fully yielded to Him." My friend, I am of the opinion that when you and I get to the end of our lives, the same will be true of you and me. It can still be said that the world has yet to see a person completely yielded to God.

So don't be discouraged with me, and I won't be discouraged with you, because, beloved, ". . . it doth not yet appear what we shall be: but we know that, when he shall appear, we shall be like him; for we shall see him as he is" (1 John 3:2). We are going to see Him some day, and then we are going to be like Him. Until then, I'll probably be very unlike Him. Maybe you will make it; I don't think I will. But in that day, I will be like Him, and at that time you are going to be delighted with me, and you are really going to love me. That is one thing that will make heaven so wonderful. Not only am I going to love everybody, but everybody is going to love me! When we get to heaven, we are going to be like Him.

"Salvation is of the LORD." This is a wonderful statement, and it is found in the Old Testament in the Book of Jonah. Do you know where this man learned that? He learned that when he was swallowed by a fish and then vomited out—then he was able to make this statement.

JONAH ARRIVES ON THE DRY LAND

And the Lord spake unto the fish, and it vomited out Jonah upon the dry land [Jonah 2:10].

I cannot resist making this corny statement: It just goes to show that you can't keep a good man down! Someone else has put it like this, "Even a fish couldn't digest Jonah, the backsliding prophet." But Jonah is a different man now. He's made some vows to God, and one of them is that he is going to Nineveh. His ticket is now to Nineveh.

CHAPTER 3

THEME: The God of the second chance; Jonah arrives in Nineveh; Nineveh believes God; Nineveh is not destroyed

Our timetable for the Book of Jonah tells us that all along Jonah's destination has been the city of Nineveh. As we come to chapter 3, his destination is still Nineveh, he leaves the dry land, and he is going to arrive in Nineveh! It has taken him three chapters, and he has had to detour through a fish, but he finally makes it. The turning around place for him was that fish—it turned him around and headed him in the right direction.

I would like to write over this third chapter the words of the Lord Jesus in His day: "For as Jonas was a sign unto the Ninevite, so shall also the Son of man be to this generation" (Luke 11:30).

THE GOD OF THE SECOND CHANCE

And the word of the LORD came unto Jonah the second time, saying [Jonah 3:1].

"The word of the LORD came unto Jonah *the second time.*" I was speaking on the Book of Jonah many years ago at a summer conference, and there was a school teacher attending the meetings. She was a lovely person, but after every session, she would come to me with a question. (School teachers always could ask me questions that I couldn't answer!) One day she asked me this question: "Suppose that after Jonah got out of the fish, he went back to Joppa and bought another ticket to go to Tarshish. What would have happened?" I had never been asked that question before, but I told her—and I still believe it—that there would have been a second fish out there waiting for him. But that wasn't necessary because Jonah had already learned his lesson. Now he was going to Nineveh—there's no question about that—he was headed for Nineveh.

I think the same thing could be said of the prodigal son. Suppose that the next year that boy had said, "Dad, stake me again. I'm going to the far country." Do you think the father would have staked him? I think he would have. The interesting thing is that the boy didn't go to the far country. Why? Because he is a son of the father, and he didn't want to get into the pigpen again. God's children may get into sin, but they surely are not going to live in sin. Pigs live in pigpens, and sons live in the father's house. It is just that simple and just that important.

"And the word of the LORD came unto Jonah the second time." Our God is the God of the second chance—what a marvelous, wonderful thing that is! God will give you a second chance, and He will give you more than that. I know that He has given me a dozen different chances. He is long-suffering and patient. He is not willing that any should perish. If you are His child, He is going to hold on to you—you may be sure of that.

Jonah now gets the call from God a second time. I do not believe that the great corporations of our day would give a man a second chance. General Motors or Standard Oil or General Foods—I have a notion that they would not give a man a second chance. Years ago here in California I became acquainted with a man who was the first vice-president of the Bank of America, which is a tremendous banking corporation. He is a very wonderful Christian and a personal friend of mine. I asked him one time, "Suppose that in one of the branches of your bank the manager absconded with all the funds, disappeared down to South America somewhere, and then, after a few years, came back and asked to be forgiven and given another chance. Would you give him a job?" He replied, "No. He's through." Such a man would not be given another chance. Isn't it wonderful that God gives us a second chance?

This is not something unusual that God did just in Jonah's case. God is not making an exception with Jonah. Remember the story of Jacob way back in the Book of Genesis? Jacob failed again and again and again and again until he actually became a disgrace to God and a source of embarrassment to Him. But God never let him go. Jacob was a trickster. He was clever. He tried to live by his own ability even when he went down to live with his Uncle Laban. Laban was smarter than

Jacob and put it over on him, but Jacob did what he could, and he did pretty well. In the end, Jacob had to flee from Laban and get out of the country. He had antagonized both his father-in-law and his brother, Esau, because of his conduct. But he could not keep on like that because he was God's man. He did want to serve God, but what a poor showing he made of it. As far as I'm concerned, I would have gotten rid of him and would have gotten someone else if I had been the Lord, but God didn't do that.

At Peniel, when Jacob came back to the land, God wrestled with him one night. Sometimes it is said that Jacob wrestled with God. Jacob didn't wrestle with God, my friend. With his father-in-law behind him and his brother ahead of him, both of them wishing Jacob dead, you may be sure of one thing: Jacob was not looking for another wrestling match! He had enough problems on his hands, and he was not about to do any wrestling. It was God who wrestled with him at Peniel. That man had to learn something that night. God crippled him before He got him, but when Jacob saw that he was losing, he finally just held on and asked for a blessing.

From that day on, Jacob was a different man. He was changed, as we can see down there in Egypt when he met his grandchildren, Joseph's sons. I'm a grandfather, and I know that a grandpa is inclined to boast just a little; you would like your grandsons to think well of you. But old Jacob didn't tell his grandsons how smart he was or how clever he was, how he put it over on Esau or how he put it over on his father-in-law Laban. This is what he did say: "May the Lord, who kept me from evil, keep the lads" (see Gen. 48:16). What a change had come over him! How humble he was. He was now resting in God, and he was a different man.

Then there is the story of David. Even today there are a great many folk who like to criticize David. One evil old man came to me with a leer in his eyes and a sneer in his voice, and he said to me, "Why did God say that David was a man after His own heart?"

I asked him, "Are you trying to stay that it was because David committed murder and adultery that God said that about him? Is that what you are trying to say?" "Well, it certainly looks that way," he said.

That man simply hadn't read the record at all. It is true that David committed an awful sin, but God punished him for it. God took him to the woodshed and whipped him within an inch of his life. Finally his heart was broken when his son Absalom was slain. That was the boy he had wanted to be king, but Absalom betrayed him. He led a rebellion against David and was murdered. How David wept! He cried, "Oh, Absalom, my son, Absalom; would to God that I had died in your stead!" (see 2 Sam. 18:33). David feared that Absalom did not know God, and so he was heartbroken the rest of his life. God punished David because of his sin, but God forgave David when he came to Him and said, "Restore unto me the joy of thy salvation . . ." (Ps. 51:12).

I went on to tell that old man who had come to me, "You know, you ought to be very glad that God said David was a man after His own heart because of his relationship with God. If God would save a man like David, He might save you, and He might save me. You ought to be thankful He's that kind of a God. He gave David a second chance, and He will give you a second and a third chance."

Simon Peter also stumbled and fell and got himself dirty. He denied Christ, and when he looked through that judgment hall, he caught the eyes of the Lord. They were not eyes looking at him in anger but in pity and in mercy. Peter went outside and wept. And then when our Lord came back from the dead, He appeared to Simon Peter privately so that Simon Peter could get things straightened out with Him.

My friend, if you are a child of God and get into sin, you can come back to Him, but you'd better mean business, and you'd better be sincere. You can go to Him and tell Him what you can tell no one else. He will accept you and receive you—He is the God of the second chance.

There is another man who failed—John Mark. He wasn't much of a missionary at first. In fact, he was chicken; he turned and went home. I once heard of a man who said that the reason he didn't fly in airplanes was because he had back trouble. When he was asked what kind of back trouble he had, he replied, "I've got a yellow streak up and down my back." John Mark had a yellow streak up and down his back—he turned and left that first missionary journey of the apostle Paul. Good old Barnabas wanted to forgive him and take him on the second missionary journey, but Paul said, "I won't take him again. I'm through with him. I'm not about to take with me anyone who turns and runs home to mama as that boy did." Paul had to change his mind later, because God will receive, and God did receive John Mark. So when Paul wrote his swan song, 2 Timothy, he said, "Take, Mark, and bring him with thee: for he is profitable to me for the ministry" (2 Tim. 4:11). John Mark made good. Aren't you glad that God gives us a second chance?

My final illustration is one not from the Bible but is very much up-to-date. Years ago here in Southern California, I was teaching the Book of Jonah on an evening radio broadcast that I had at that time. A day or two after I had enlarged on this first verse of the third chapter, I received a letter from a medical doctor in Beverly Hills, California. He said, "I want you to know that this verse is now the most important verse in the Bible to me. When you said that God is the God of the second chance, I came back to Him." He went on in his letter to tell me his story. He had come from Chicago where he had been a prominent doctor and also an officer in the church. Problems arose in the church which involved the handling of property and funds. He was blamed for the problems, although he was not guilty and had not been involved at all. He became bitter and actually left the Chicago area. He came to California and established an office here, but he never would darken the door of a church. He did, however, listen to me on the radio. When I said that God is a God of the second chance, this man wrote that "it was just like a cool drink of water to a man who was out on the desert, dying of thirst. That meant more to me than anything." I sat down and wrote that man a letter, and I did what any preacher would do—I urged him to get into a church and to get busy again for the Lord. He wrote again and said, "I'm already back in church and busy for the Lord." God is the God of the second chance, my friend; He is wonderful.

Jonah's story is an illustration of how God treats His children when they sin and come back to Him. The prodigal son came home. When he came home, he didn't get a beating; he got a banquet. He didn't get kicked around; he got kisses. Instead of the poor boy being put out of the house and rejected, the father took the boy back. How wonderful this is!

JONAH ARRIVES IN NINEVEH

Now we are going to see how God is gracious to a sinful city. This is a record of perhaps the greatest revival in the history of the world; that is, what we call a revival—people turning to God. What happened in Nineveh makes the Day of Pentecost look very small. A few thousand turned to God on the Day of Pentecost, but there were several hundred thousand in the city of Nineveh who turned to God. There has never been anything quite like it—an entire city turned to God! No one else has ever seen that happen. The apostle Paul never stayed in a city until everyone was converted; he just preached the Word and moved on to the next town. No one from that day down to the present has seen such a moving of the Spirit of God as took place in Nineveh so long ago.

It is interesting to note that all this happened in Nineveh before the church arrived on the scene, and the greatest revival of all time will take place *after* the church leaves the earth. You see, God is simply not dependent upon the church. If you have the notion that the church or your church or your group are the only ones God has ever had in mind, I say to you very candidly that it is a false notion. God has something even bigger in mind than the church. Now the church is to be the bride of Christ and will, I think, occupy the very closest place to the Son of God throughout eternity, but God had a purpose in mind before the church got here and even before man appeared on this earth. God was not sitting around, twiddling His thumbs and waiting for man to come along, my friend!

Today His purpose is to call out a people from every tribe, tongue, and nation. We believe that we are coming to the end of the age and that God wants the Word to go out so that everyone might hear. However, the greatest revival, the greatest turning to God, is yet in the future, and the story of Nineveh is just a small adumbration of that.

Arise, go unto Nineveh, that great city, and preach unto it the preaching that I bid thee [Jonah 3:2].

We have been told before that this city of Nineveh was a great city (see Jonah 1:2), and the last verse of the book of Jonah also says, "And should not I spare Nineveh, that great city, wherein are more than six-score thousand persons that cannot discern between their right hand and their left hand; and also much cattle?" (Jonah 4:11). The unbeliever has criticized the Book of Jonah on many counts, and one of them is the fact that three times in this book it says that Nineveh was a great city, an exceeding great city. The Ninevites were great in sin, to be sure, but they also had a very large city.

However, nothing was known about Nineveh until 1845 when Sir Austen Layard was the first to examine the ruins of this city; he and George Smith excavated the ancient city of Nineveh. Nineveh proper, that is, the tell of Nineveh, was across the Tigris River from the modern city of Mosul. It was built in the shape of a trapezium, which was about two and one-half miles in length and a mile and one-third in breadth. That would make it a pretty good-sized place, but I would say very frankly that that does not meet the demands of the Book of Jonah.

The city of Nineveh lay in a plain which was almost entirely surrounded by rivers. The Tigris River came along to a point at which the Upper Zab River ran into it, forming a V-shaped valley between the two rivers. Then across the top of them, at the north, there was a range of mountains. This entire area, therefore, was protected by the natural fortifications of the rivers and the mountains. There were several prominent cities in this natural enclosure. Nineveh was located up on the Tigris River. Down at the fork where the Upper Zab flowed into the Tigris was Calah, as it is called in Scripture, now known as the Nimrud ruins. Calah was eighteen miles southeast of Nineveh proper. The city of Khorsabad was twelve miles to the northeast of Nineveh on the Upper Zab River.

This statement by Jonah that Nineveh was a great city sounds strange for a day when cities were walled and were by necessity very compact and small. What surprises many folk when they go to Jerusalem is the fact that the walled city is so small. It was even smaller in Christ's day and certainly in David's day than it is today. The walled city of ancient days was very compact. It was really a fortress for the people to come into in time of siege. In Nineveh there were really three walled cities—Nineveh proper, Calah, and Khorsabad. Nineveh became the capital, and the entire area was known by its name. In that fertile valley, then, there lived a great multitude of folk who in time of siege would go into these cities. They tell us that one of the reasons Nineveh fell was not primarily because of the enemy from the outside, but because of a flood that took out one whole section of the wall of the city.

It is quite interesting that when we go back to the Book of Genesis, we read this: "Out of that land went forth Asshur, and builded Nineveh, and the city Rehoboth, and Calah, and Resen between Nineveh and Calah: the same is a great city" (Gen. 10:11–12). All the way through the Word of God, the greatness of this city is emphasized. All of this area was given the name of Nineveh because it was the capital.

One of the ancient writers, Ctesias, describes Nineveh as a city whose circuit is 480 stadia. This would mean that its circumference was over twenty-seven miles.

So we find that Nineveh was "an exceeding great city" with one community after another. Here in Southern California we have a situation very similar to Nineveh's. The Los Angeles area includes at least twenty-five smaller municipalities besides the actual city of Los Angeles. We speak of all of them as being a part of "the greater Los Angeles area," which covers a great deal of ground. In fact, the joke during World War II was that a soldier who got lost up in Alaska and was trying to find his way back finally came to a sign that said, LOS ANGELES CITY LIMITS, and he knew he was no longer lost!

Nineveh was a great city—great in size and great in wickedness. This city was guilty of the same sins, which we read about in the other prophetic books, that brought God's judgment. In the Books of Amos and Hosea, we find that the reason God brought judgment upon the people was because of their luxurious living and sexual immorality, because of their godless music, and because of their drunkenness. The same things could be said of Nineveh. They were given over to idolatry, their cruelty and brutality to their enemies were unspeakable, and there was gross immorality in the city. It was a city of wine and women, of the bottle and the brothel, of sauce and sex. These were the things that identified the great city of Nineveh.

It is into this great city that Jonah is now called to go and to minister.

> **So Jonah arose, and went unto Nineveh, according to the word of the LORD. Now Nineveh was an exceeding great city of three days' journey [Jonah 3:3].**

Notice that Jonah is now doing things "according to the word of the LORD." The first time he had set sail for Tarshish, which was *not* according to the word of the Lord; now he is going into Nineveh according to the word of the Lord.

"Now Nineveh was an exceeding great city of three days' journey." This, of course, is the statement which caused the critics to laugh and to ridicule. The fact of the matter is, as we have explained, it would take several hours to go through just one of these cities, but there were three cities as well as a great area between them in which was a population estimated at several million. It is into this area that Jonah is now coming. It was "an exceeding great city of three days' journey."

> **And Jonah began to enter into the city a day's journey, and he cried, and said, Yet forty days, and Nineveh shall be overthrown [Jonah 3:4].**

The point is that it took Jonah quite a while to cover this ground. He didn't have radio, he didn't even have a loud speaker—and I've often wondered how he did it. I think of Nineveh's similarity to the Los Angeles area. I live in a city called Pasadena, about ten miles from downtown Los Angeles. To the south of Pasadena about twenty-five miles is Long Beach, and to the west about twenty miles is Santa Monica. All in between there is just one city after another. Imagine Jonah starting out walking here in Southern California (he didn't have a car, by the way). He would stop at a street corner, a busy intersection, and give his message. Then he would move on down the street to another intersection and, while he was waiting for the traffic signal to change, he would speak to another crowd. In this manner it would take him quite some time to get through a city.

At this point someone is going to ask me, "How did Jonah get a crowd?" Drawing a crowd is always a problem for a preacher. It's natural and normal for us to want as many people as possible to hear the Word of God. How did Jonah do it? He didn't use any of our modern methods or our modern tactics. He didn't rent a great auditorium and put on a great campaign—there's nothing wrong with that; in fact, that's very right to do today—but Jonah didn't do it. He didn't use any gimmicks. He didn't bring in celebrities or some great singer. He didn't entertain the crowd. That was not his method.

Jonah used a method that is a little different from any that we could use today. His method was that he was a man from the dead, and I think he was rather spectacular to see. A man who has spent three days and three nights in a fish simply cannot come out looking like he did when he went in!

If you recall the illustrations which I gave earlier of the men who had been swallowed by a fish and lived to tell the story, you will remember that the late Dr. Harry Rimmer told about seeing one man who had spent two days inside a fish. The man was put on display in London as "the Jonah of the twentieth century." When Dr. Rimmer interviewed him two years after it had happened, this man didn't have a hair on his body, and his skin was a yellowish-brown color. You see, the gastric juices of the fish had reacted upon the individual as the fish had tried to digest him.

Those chemicals were bound to have an effect upon him, and this is apparently what happened to Jonah also. You can imagine the color of Jonah's skin, and you can imagine how he must have looked. When he stopped at a corner and the crowd gathered, they would say, "Brother, where have you been?" Jonah told them, "I am a man from the dead. A fish swallowed me because God had sent me to Nineveh but I tried to run away to Tarshish." People didn't ridicule Jonah's story. They listened to him.

I am told that in Russia today, out through the rural areas, there is a great company of people who have turned to the Lord. On one of our tours to Bible lands, I went ahead of the group and was fortunate to go through Belgrade, Yugoslavia. There was a mix-up about the time we were to be there, but I understand that there were some five hundred Christians who were going to be there to welcome us had they known our arrival time. This happened because some of our tapes are being translated into Yugoslavian, Romanian, and several other languages and are being used by folk there today. There is a real moving of the spirit of God in places where we would not expect it.

Who would have thought that in the wicked city of Nineveh people would listen to the Word of God and to a man who said, "I'm back from the dead"? By the way, that is the same message we have. We have a message concerning a man who came back from the dead. Paul writes, ". . . if we believe on him that raised up Jesus our Lord from the dead; who was delivered for our offences, and was raised again for our justification" (Rom. 4:24–25).

Jonah entered the city with a message of judgment: "Yet forty days, and Nineveh shall be overthrown." I think Jonah gave that message with relish—he didn't like Ninevites!

NINEVEH BELIEVES GOD

So the people of Nineveh believed God, and proclaimed a fast, and put on sackcloth, from the greatest of them even to the least of them [Jonah 3:5].

"So the people of Nineveh believed God"—that is a marvelous statement to find in the Old Testament. All God has ever asked any person, any sinner, to do is simply to believe Him. What does He ask you to believe? Believe what He has done for you. Believe that Christ died for you—that He died for you and for your sins. Believe that He was raised again and is now at God's right hand. The people of Nineveh believed God—that is still the important thing today.

I am afraid that we have in our churches many people who are as busy as termites—they take little courses, and they talk a great deal about the Bible—but they do not know God. I was speaking with a man the other day who is that type of an individual; he goes to everything that comes along. I had gotten a little weary of hearing him tell about where he'd been and what he'd seen. He has done very little, but he is always telling about the great meetings he attends. I asked him pointblank, "Do you *believe* God?" He thought for a minute and then said, "Well, I think I do." May I say to you, all of his work is of no value because he does not really believe God.

"So the people of Nineveh believed God, and proclaimed a fast." They *demonstrated* their belief. Faith always leads to works. "And put on sackcloth, from the greatest of them even to the least of them."

For word came unto the king of Nineveh, and he arose from his throne, and he laid his robe from him, and covered him with sackcloth, and sat in ashes [Jonah 3:6].

Friend, when people start doing these things they no longer will be committing sin. They are in deep repentance before God and are asking God for mercy. And when you ask God for mercy, you are going to find out that He is merciful.

And he caused it to be proclaimed and published through Nineveh by the decree of the king and his nobles, saying, Let neither man nor beast, herd nor flock, taste any thing: let them not feed, nor drink water [Jonah 3:7].

These people, many of whom were alcoholics, are now told not even to drink water.

But let man and beast be covered with sackcloth, and cry mightily unto God: yea, let them turn every one from his evil way, and from the violence that is in their hands [Jonah 3:8].

You, also, must turn from sin, my friend. If you come to Christ, you can come just as you are, but when you come, you will turn from sin. You cannot possibly accept Him and not turn from sin.

"Let them turn every one from his evil way, and from the violence that is in their hands." The Ninevites were a brutal and violent people.

They were given to riots. They were given to cruelty and brutality and mob rule. Now the king says, "Turn from all of that and cry to God for mercy."

The strangest thing happened—the whole city turned to God! Now that was remarkable; in fact, it was quite amazing. From the king on the throne to the peasant in the hovel, they all turned to the Lord. They cried mightily to God, and they believed God. What a glorious, wonderful time this was!

We hear today that we are having revival in certain places. I do not think that you can call what is taking place anywhere (certainly not in the United States) a revival. I do think we are seeing a great moving of the Spirit of God in certain places. Wherever the Word of God is preached and taught, you will see a moving of the Spirit of God; but we are not seeing revival. Instead, we find that the church is quite inactive as far as getting out the Word of God, winning people to Christ, and building them up in the faith.

When I speak of the church, I mean you and me, all of us who are believers, regardless of the group with which we are identified or the local assembly to which we go. Someone sent me this little quote because he had heard me say that there are a great many church members who are not real believers. Here it is: "Church members are either pillars or caterpillars. The pillars hold up the church; the caterpillars just crawl in and out." That's accurate, my friend. That is our problem today. We have too many caterpillars and not enough pillars to hold up the church.

NINEVEH IS NOT DESTROYED

Jonah went to the city of Nineveh, and the entire city turned to God. This was something that had never happened before. Certainly Noah didn't have this kind of experience!—but Jonah did. What will God do now that the city has turned to Him? The king himself asks the question—

Who can tell if God will turn and repent, and turn away from his fierce anger, that we perish not?

**And God saw their works, that they turned from their
evil way; and God repented of the evil, that he had said
that he would do unto them; and he did it not [Jonah
3:9–10].**

We have come to what is probably the strongest statement in Scripture
about God repenting. What does it mean when Scripture says that
God repented? Does God repent? The word *repentance* as it is used in
both the Old and New Testaments primarily means "a change of
mind." In the Septuagint (the Greek translation of the Old Testament),
the word is *metanoesen*, meaning "to change your mind." The question arises then: *Does God change His mind?*

     One of the attributes of God is that He is immutable, which means
that He never changes. There is no reason for God to change. He
knows the end from the beginning. When the *Los Angeles Times* came
out this morning, it didn't tell God a thing. God has not learned anything from the politicians or from our colleges today—they haven't
taught Him anything. God knows the end from the beginning, and
there is no reason for Him to change His mind. He is carrying on the
program that He outlined at the beginning, and He is simply following through on it. Therefore, God does not change.

     But Scripture does say that God repents. Follow me carefully here:
There are expressions used in the Word of God which are called anthropomorphic terms; that is, there are certain attributes of man
which are ascribed to God. In the Bible certain physical and psychological attributes of man are attributed to God.

     First of all, let us look at some physical attributes of mankind that
are ascribed to God. It says in Scripture that ". . . the *eyes* of the LORD
run to and fro throughout the whole earth . . ." (2 Chron. 16:9, italics
mine). Does that mean that God has eyes like I have? If He does, are
they blue or brown or gray eyes? God is a spirit, and He does not have
eyes like we have. But the one who made the eye can see, and He can
see *without* the eye. The Lord knew that Vernon McGee would have a
problem understanding that, and so He said, "The eyes of the LORD
run to and fro throughout the whole earth." I can understand that
now—that means that God sees everything. That is an anthropomor-

phic term, ascribing to God an attribute that belongs to man in order
that we can understand.

The Bible also speaks of the *arm* of the Lord and the *hand* of the
Lord. That is very helpful to my understanding, but the one who made
my hand and my arm does not have a hand or an arm like I have because God is a spirit. But the Bible says, "The heavens declare the
glory of God; and the firmament sheweth his handiwork" (Ps. 19:1)—
that really means *finger* work. John Wesley put it like this: "God created the heavens and the earth, and He didn't even half try." Finger
work is like crocheting or knitting; it doesn't require a great deal of
muscle. You don't have to do sitting up exercises for six months before
you can learn to knit. God created the heavens and the earth—that is
His finger work.

However, when Isaiah was speaking of God's salvation and His redemption, he said, "Who hath believed our report? and to whom is
the [bared] arm of the LORD revealed?" (Isa. 53:1, italics mine). I understand now what I would not have understood before: It cost God
more, and it was more difficult for Him to redeem man than it was for
Him to create a universe.

These are examples of anthropomorphic terms, of physical attributes of man being attributed to God for the sake of our understanding.
The Scriptures also attribute certain psychological attributes of man
to God. For example, the *anger* of the Lord. Does God get angry? He
surely does. He is angry with the wicked all of the time. God can get
angry, but His anger is not like my anger. I get angry when I hear that
someone has said something bad about me, but that doesn't bother
God at all. His anger is not peevish or petulant but is an anger that is
against all wickedness and sin.

Scripture tells us that God *loves,* and that is something I can understand. In fact, in the little Book of Ruth, God takes a very human
relationship—the love of a man for a woman—as a picture of His love
for us. Also, the church is called the bride of Christ. That tells us
something of the love of God. God loves you, and you cannot keep
Him from loving you.

Here in Jonah we have another example: God *repents.* To repent
means to change your mind; that is what it means when it applies to

me. When I repent, I change my mind. I did something wrong, and I now see that it was wrong. I turn from it, and I go to God and ask forgiveness for it—I come over on God's side. To confess your sin is to come over and agree with God about your sin.

But does God repent like that? Does He change His mind? Does He say, "My, I made a mistake there; I shouldn't destroy Nineveh"? No. We need to see that the city of Nineveh had two options when this man Jonah entered it with his message of judgment. They could reject God's message, they could ignore it, they could pay no attention to it, and if they did, they would be destroyed—God's never changed that. Or they could accept God's message, they could turn to Him, and God would deliver and save them. God is immutable—He never changes. When His Word is rejected, when people turn from Him, they are lost. But when they turn to Him, He will always save them, regardless of who they are.

Therefore, *who* changed? Did God change? No, but it looked as if He did. Jonah had said, "Yet forty days, and this city is going to be destroyed. God is going to destroy it." But God did not destroy Nineveh. Did God break His Word? No. God is the same yesterday, today, and forever. The city had two options. If they had not accepted His Word, they would have been destroyed. But they *did* accept God's message, they believed God, and they turned from their wickedness. God didn't change; He will always save people when they turn to Him. Although it looked as if God changed, it was really the city of Nineveh that changed, and that makes all the difference in the world.

CHAPTER 4

THEME: Jonah's displeasure; God's gracious dealing
with Jonah

This fourth chapter is like an addendum to the Book of Jonah, because at the end of chapter 3 the mission is accomplished. As you know, I arranged each chapter of this book according to a timetable. In chapter 1, Jonah left the northern kingdom of Israel, probably from Gath-hepher, his hometown. His destination was Nineveh, and it took him three chapters to get there. But he accomplished his mission, and the entire city turned to God. It would seem that the book ought to end there. But the problem no longer is Nineveh—the problem now is Jonah. Jonah was a problem child. God had more trouble with a backsliding prophet by the name of Jonah than He had with an entire city of brutal, cruel, pagan sinners.

If I had had the privilege of being the one who brought God's message to Nineveh and had seen the result that Jonah saw, I believe that I would have gone down to the Western Union office and sent a telegram back to my hometown. I would want to tell people what had happened and cause them to praise and thank God for what had been accomplished. I would rejoice in it, but that is because of where I am and because I am under altogether different circumstances. If I had been in Jonah's shoes, if I had been in Jonah's fish, I might have had the same feeling that he did. Yet his reaction is something that seems unbelievable. In fact, I have no problem with the fish, but I have a lot of problems with this man Jonah. At the very beginning, he was called to go in one direction, and he headed in the other direction. I don't understand that—until I look closely at my own heart and see that I have headed in the wrong direction several times when it was very clear that God wanted me to go in the opposite direction.

Jonah now has a new destination. He is going to leave Nineveh, and he is glad to get out of town. His destination now is a gourd vine or, as I would like to imagine, a trailer court outside the city. Jonah goes out of the city and finds himself a little spot where he can park his camper for awhile. As he leaves Nineveh, his destination is a little spot outside the city, and he is going to arrive in the heart of God. I do not know of a better place for anybody to arrive than in the heart of God, and that is where this prophet is going to arrive.

God is going to seek to win Jonah over to His viewpoint. This chapter will demonstrate to us the fact that God will never interfere with your free will. He is not going to force you on any issue whatsoever, for you are a free moral agent. God has actually moved heaven and hell and has come by way of a cross to knock at your heart's door. But, my friend, He will not come any farther than that until that door is opened, and it must be opened from the inside. He will never crash the door of your heart; He will never push it in; He will never come in uninvited. God is now going to have to deal with a backsliding prophet who has a pretty strong will and who hates Ninevites. He is going to try to win Jonah over to His viewpoint.

JONAH'S DISPLEASURE

But it displeased Jonah exceedingly, and he was very angry [Jonah 4:1].

It didn't simply displease Jonah a little bit; it displeased him *exceedingly*. He wasn't angry just a little bit; he was *very* angry. What is this man angry about? He's angry because the city of Nineveh turned to God—he didn't like that.

And he prayed unto the LORD, and said, I pray thee, O LORD, was not this my saying, when I was yet in my country? Therefore I fled before unto Tarshish: for I knew that thou art a gracious God, and merciful, slow to anger, and of great kindness, and repentest thee of the evil [Jonah 4:2].

"And he prayed unto the LORD"—the last time Jonah prayed he was inside the fish. Here he is outside of Nineveh, with his camper parked up there in a little trailer court, and as he sits in the shade of it, he prays. He's very unhappy; in fact, he's miserable.

You may have felt that I was inaccurate in the Introduction when I said that Jonah had hatred and bitterness in his heart against the Ninevites, that he probably had justification for it, and that it was one of the reasons he did not want to go to Nineveh. But listen to him now: "O LORD, was not this my saying, when I was yet in my country? Therefore I fled before unto Tarshish: for I knew that thou art a gracious God, and merciful, slow to anger, and of great kindness, and repentest thee of the evil."

Years ago I heard a liberal lecturing at Vanderbilt University who said that Jonah's problem was that he did not know God. I don't like to say it like this, but the problem with that lecturer was that he didn't know the Book of Jonah. It is very clear that Jonah did know God and that he knew Him very well, probably better than that lecturer knew God. Jonah says to God, "I knew You were gracious, I knew You were merciful, I knew You were slow to anger, and I knew You were of great kindness. And I knew that although You said You would destroy Nineveh in forty days, if Nineveh would turn to You, You would save them because that's what You always do." Jonah knew God and, knowing God, he said, "I hate Ninevites. I don't want them saved. I want God to judge them." So he had headed in the opposite direction from Nineveh. Jonah said, "If those Ninevites would turn to God, God would save them, and you just can't depend on Ninevites—they might put up a good front. They might say that they've turned to God." Jonah should have known that God knew their hearts and knew whether they were genuine or not. But Jonah did know how merciful and good and gracious God is.

Jonah is in great bitterness and anger. Listen to him—

Therefore now, O LORD, take, I beseech thee, my life from me; for it is better for me to die than to live [Jonah 4:3].

Two of the great prophets of Scripture said the same thing, that they wanted God to take their lives. In other words, they were actually on the verge of suicide. When the prophet Elijah ran from Jezebel—another man running away, and it was unlike him—he went all the way to Beer-sheba, which was the jumping-off place for the Sinai Peninsula. Elijah left his servant there and kept on going as long as he could. When he was out of breath, he crawled up under a juniper tree and he said, "Oh, Lord, let me die!" When God's man does that, that man is exhausted and drained physically, mentally, psychologically, and spiritually. Every drop is drained out of him. That was true of Elijah. He had been busy, and I mean busy, friend! He had withstood the prophets of Baal way up at Mount Carmel. He had been before the public. Although Elijah loved the spectacular and he loved the dramatic, it drained him after awhile. So when he heard that Jezebel was after him, he simply took out for the far country.

Now I think you'll agree that Jonah has really been through the mill—in fact, he's been through a fish. He had quite an experience. Then he came into the city of Nineveh, he gave out God's Word faithfully, and the city turned to God. This man is now overwrought, overstimulated. He is exhausted, absolutely drained—and he wants to die. Many of us reach this stage sometimes. We get to the place where we feel like saying, "This is it. I give up. I quit. I don't want to go any farther." We're tired; we're exhausted. But to wish that you were dead is just about as foolish a thing as you can possibly do. As far as I know, no one has ever died by wishing. People die of cancer, of heart trouble, and of all kinds of things, but they just don't die of *wishing* to be dead. Jonah is wasting his time.

GOD'S GRACIOUS DEALING WITH JONAH

Notice how graciously God deals with this man—

> **Then said the LORD, Doest thou well to be angry? [Jonah 4:4].**

Dr. G. Douglas Young has given us what I believe is a much better translation here. He has translated it like this: "Is doing good displeasing to you?"—that's what God meant. God says, "Jonah, I have saved Nineveh because I'm in the saving business and I save sinners. I wanted you to bring them the message of judgment to see whether or not they would turn to Me. If they turned to Me, I would save them. They did turn to Me, and I have saved them." My friend, if there is joy in heaven over one sinner turning to God, they must have had a real big time up there when all the folk in Nineveh turned to God. God asks Jonah, "Is this displeasing to you that I have saved these Ninevites?"

Jonah is in a huff, and he's pouting. Notice what he does—

So Jonah went out of the city, and sat on the east side of the city, and there made him a booth, and sat under it in the shadow, till he might see what would become of the city [Jonah 4:5].

"So Jonah went out of the city, and sat on the east side of the city." The east side of the city was up in the hill country, up at an elevation. Jonah got himself a good spot where he could look out over the city. Why? Because he didn't trust the Ninevites. He thought they would go right back into their sinning; and if they did, he knew God would destroy them because God never changes. Jonah wanted to be up there if the fire fell. That's the kind of man we are dealing with here—and he's the man who had brought God's message.

"And there made him a booth, and sat under it in the shadow, till he might see what would become of the city." He didn't believe Nineveh would stick by their conversion, their confession of faith. He's up there, and he's waiting for the fire of God's judgment to fall.

God is now going to move in on this man Jonah, and He's going to deal with him personally. We are going to have an answer here to the question that is often asked: Do you have to love people before you can bring the Word of God to them? Do you have to love a people before you can go as a missionary to them? Jonah may be a good example in this particular connection, for one thing is sure: Jonah didn't love the Ninevites.

And the LORD God prepared a gourd, and made it to come up over Jonah, that it might be a shadow over his

head, to deliver him from his grief. So Jonah was exceeding glad of the gourd [Jonah 4:6].

"And the LORD God prepared a gourd." This gourd was prepared in the same way that God prepared the fish. If you don't believe in the fish, you ought not to believe in the gourd. I believe in the gourd; I believe in the fish.

"And made it to come up over Jonah, that it might be a shadow over his head, to deliver him from his grief. So Jonah was exceeding glad of the gourd." Jonah is made happy at last by this little green gourd growing up. Every day Jonah would go down to the Tigris River, fill a bucket with water, and come up and water this gourd that was growing in that dry country. He trained it to run up over his camper, you know. He sat under the shade of it, and he became very attached to it.

If we understand a little about human nature, we can understand Jonah a little better. It is amazing how people can get attached to living things other than human beings, especially if they are lonely. If they have no person to love, they will have a dog or cat or even a vine to love. Several years ago I visited a friend in Chicago who lived in an apartment. She had several plants, and one of them was a geranium. She took me over to show me the geranium which was just a little old stub sticking up out of the pot. In my yard in Pasadena I have to cut back the geraniums with a hoe in order to keep them from taking over! But this lady said to me, "Dr. McGee, look here at this little geranium. I know you grow them in California, but this one is such a sweet one. It grows up each year and has flowers on it. It dies back in wintertime, although the apartment is warm—I don't know why it does that." I told her. "Well, geraniums have a habit of lunging out in a spurt of growth at times." But hers hadn't done much lunging, you can be sure of that—it was just a little, bitty thing. As we walked away, she *patted* that little geranium and said, "You sweet little thing, you!" I thought, *My gracious, does she talk to the geranium?* I guess she did. She certainly was a very sensible and intelligent woman, but she lived alone and really did not have many friends.

Jonah has no friends, he doesn't like Ninevites, and there's not a person in that city whom he cares about visiting. He's alone, and he's out of fellowship with God at this time. So God lets him get attached to a little old gourd. I have a notion that Jonah would come panting up the hill with a bucket of water every afternoon and would say to the gourd, "Little gourd, I've brought you your drink for today." Can you imagine that? Well, people can get attached to dogs in that way also. One evening when my daughter was just a little thing, I took her for a walk. We came to a corner where there were a lot of vines, and we couldn't see around the corner, but we could hear a woman talking. I have never heard such sweet talk in my life! I thought we were interrupting a romance; so I took my daughter and started to cross the street. But then the woman came around the corner, and she was carrying a little dog. Imagine talking to a dog like that! I do not know if she was married or not, but if she was, I'll bet that her husband wasn't hearing sweet talk like that. We speak of some people leading "a dog's life"—there are some men who wish they could lead a dog's life! Jonah talked that way to this gourd vine—he's attached to it!

Watch how God is going to move in on Jonah—

But God prepared a worm when the morning rose the next day, and it smote the gourd that it withered [Jonah 4:7].

"But God prepared a worm"—this worm is just as miraculous as the fish. "And it smote the gourd that it withered." This worm cut the vine down because worms just don't fall in love with gourds—they like to eat them.

And it came to pass, when the sun did arise, that God prepared a vehement east wind; and the sun beat upon the head of Jonah, that he fainted, and wished in himself to die, and said, It is better for me to die than to live [Jonah 4:8].

Here he goes again, *wishing*—but it won't do him a bit of good.

> **And God said to Jonah, Doest thou well to be angry for the gourd? And he said, I do well to be angry, even unto death [Jonah 4:9].**

Jonah says, "The only thing that I had that was living and that I cared for was this little gourd vine that grew up here and that You gave to me. And now the worm has cut the thing down, and here I am all alone."

> **Then said the LORD, Thou hast had pity on the gourd, for the which thou hast not laboured, neither madest it grow; which came up in a night, and perished in a night [Jonah 4:10].**

God says to Jonah, "Jonah, a gourd is nothing." My friend, I hate to say this, but a pussycat is nothing, a little dog is nothing, but a human being has a soul that is either going to heaven or hell. And God didn't ask you to *love* the lost before you go to them. He said, "I love the lost, and I want you to go to them." That is what He is saying to Jonah: "Jonah, I love the Ninevites."

> **And should not I spare Nineveh, that great city, wherein are more than sixscore thousand persons that cannot discern between their right hand and their left hand; and also much cattle? [Jonah 4:11].**

God says, "I have spared this city." What does He mean by "sixscore thousand [120,000] persons that cannot discern between their right hand and their left hand"? He means little children. God says, "You wouldn't want Me to destroy that city, would you, Jonah? If you can fall in love with a gourd vine, can't you at least fall in love with Ninevite children?"

Now may I make this application? When I was teaching in a Bible institute, I used to say, like all the other teachers were saying, that if you are called to go as a missionary, you ought to love the people to whom you go. I disagree violently with that now, because how can you love people before you know them? I first applied that to myself. I have never accepted a call to a church because I loved the people; I didn't know them to begin with. I went because I felt that God had called me to go there and preach. But I also have never been in a church in which I didn't become involved with the people. I have stood at their bedsides in hospitals, I've been at their gravesides when death came, I've been with them in the marriages that have taken place in their families, and I can truthfully say that I have never yet left a church where there wasn't a great company of people whom I loved—and I really mean that I love them in the Lord. But I did not love them when I went there because I did not know them.

God is saying to a great many people today, "I want you to go and take the Word of God to those who are lost." And they say, "But I don't love them." God says, "I never asked you to love them; I asked you to go." I cannot find anywhere that God ever asked Jonah to go because he loved the Ninevites. He said, "Jonah, I want you to go because I love them. I love Ninevites. I want to save Ninevites. And I want you to take the message to them."

Again may I say that I am afraid there are a great many people in the church who are caterpillars. Church members are either pillars or caterpillars; the pillars hold up the church, and the caterpillars just crawl in and out. There are a lot of people just crawling in and out of the church, waiting for some great wave of emotion, waiting for some feeling to take hold of them—and they have never done anything yet. God says that we are to get busy for Him.

I remember talking to a missionary who was home from Africa, and he was showing me a picture of some little black boys in the orphans' home there. I could tell by the way he looked at the picture that he loved those little boys. I said to him, "When you first went to Africa, did you love the Africans?" He said, "No, I really wanted to go to my people in Greece, but at that time the door was closed, and I could not go; so I had to go to Africa." As he held that picture, I said to him, "But do you love those little fellows now?" Tears came down from his eyes. He said, "I love them now." God says to you and me, "You go with the Word. I love the lost. You take the Word to them, and when they are saved and you get acquainted with them and know them, you will love them, too."

Since Jonah wrote the book, I think it is reasonable to say that after this experience, Jonah left the dead gourd vine and went down to where the living were walking the streets of Nineveh, and I think that he rejoiced with them that they had come to a saving knowledge of God. My friend, what a message this is! Why don't you get involved in getting the Word of God out to people? Don't wait for some great feeling to sweep over your soul. Don't wait to be moved by a little picture of an orphan. There are so many people waiting to be motivated by things that are emotional. Take the Word of God to them because God loves them; and if you'll do that, I will guarantee that you will learn to love them also.

BIBLIOGRAPHY
(Recommended for Further Study)

Feinberg, Charles L. *The Minor Prophets*. Chicago, Illinois: Moody Press, 1976.

Gaebelein, Arno C. *The Annotated Bible*. 1917. Reprint. Neptune, New Jersey: Loizeaux Brothers, 1971.

Ironside. H. A. *The Minor Prophets*. Neptune, New Jersey: Loizeaux Brothers, n.d.

Jensen, Irving L. *Minor Prophets of Judah*. Chicago, Illinois: Moody Press, 1975.

Tatford, Frederick A. *The Minor Prophets*. Minneapolis, Minnesota: Klock & Klock, n.d.

Unger, Merrill F. *Unger's Commentary on the Old Testament*, Vol. 2. Chicago, Illinois: Moody Press, 1982.

MICAH

The Book of
MICAH
INTRODUCTION

It is important to know something about the man Micah as well as his message. His name means "who is like Jehovah?" The word has the same derivation as Michael (the name of the archangel) which means "who is like God?" There are many Micahs mentioned in the Scriptures, but this man is identified as a Morasthite (Mic. 1:1), since he was an inhabitant of Moresheth-gath (Mic. 1:14), a place about twenty miles southwest of Jerusalem, near Lachish. He is not to be confused with any other Micah of Scripture.

Micah prophesied during the reigns of Jotham, Ahaz, and Hezekiah (see Mic. 1:1), who were kings of Judah. However, his prophecy concerns Samaria and Jerusalem. Samaria was the capital of the northern kingdom of Israel, while Jerusalem was the capital of the southern kingdom of Judah. Although he was a man from the southern kingdom, a great deal of his prophecy had to do with the northern kingdom. He spoke to the nation during the time that the northern kingdom was being attacked by Assyria. Although the southern kingdom was attacked also, it was the northern kingdom that actually was carried away into Assyrian captivity.

Micah was a contemporary of three other prophets: Isaiah, Hosea, and Amos. It is possible that he was a friend of Isaiah, and his prophecy has been called that of a miniature Book of Isaiah. There are many striking similarities between the two. For many people, Micah is the favorite of the minor prophets. It is one of the most remarkable books as to style. If you appreciate beautiful language, if you appreciate poetry, and if you appreciate literature, you will appreciate Micah.

The writing is pungent, and personal. Micah was trenchant, touching, and tender. He was realistic and reportorial—he would have made a good war correspondent. There is an exquisite beauty about this brochure which combines God's infinite tenderness with His judgments. There are several famous passages which are familiar to the average Christian, although he may not recognize them as coming from Micah. Through the gloom of impending judgment, Micah saw clearly the coming glory of the redemption of Israel, which makes this a remarkable book.

Micah pronounced judgment on the cities of Israel and on Jerusalem in Judah. These centers influenced the people of the nation. These were the urban problems that sound very much like our present-day problems. Micah condemned violence, corruption, robbery, covetousness, gross materialism, spiritual bankruptcy, and illicit sex. He well could be labeled "the prophet of the city."

The theme of Micah is very important to understand. Customarily, Micah is considered a prophet of judgment. That seems to be true since in the first three chapters there is a great emphasis on judgment. However, although the first three chapters are denunciatory, the last four chapters are consolatory. His great question is found in one of the loveliest passages of Scripture. "Who is like unto Thee?" that is, unto God. We find that Micah emphasizes that theme as he goes along. In the first thee chapters: Who is like unto God in proclaiming—that is, in witnessing? In chapters 4 and 5: Who is like unto God in prophesying, in consoling? In chapter 6: Who is like unto God in pleading? Finally, in chapter 7: Who is like unto God in pardoning? This is what makes Micah a wonderful little book. The main theme of the book is God's judgment and redemption—both are there. The key verse, to me, is Micah 7:18 which says, "Who is a God like unto thee, that pardoneth iniquity, and passeth by the transgression of the remnant of his heritage? he retaineth not his anger for ever, because he delighteth in mercy."

God hates sin, but He loves the souls of sinners, and He wants to save them. Judgment is called God's "strange work." It is strange because He does not like to judge. But since He is a holy God and hates sin, He must deal with any rebellion. He couldn't do otherwise. But

He still loves the souls of sinners: He wants to save them, and He will save them if they come to Him in faith.

This little book can be divided in an interesting way. The more natural division of the prophecy is to note that Micah gave three messages, each beginning with the injunction, "Hear" (Mic. 1:2, 3:1; 6:1). The first message is addressed to "all people," and the second message is addressed specifically to the leaders of Israel. The third message is a personal word of pleading to Israel to repent and return to God.

Now let me refer briefly to the attack upon the unity of this book by the German higher critics of many years ago. They made the same attack which they made upon the prophecy of Isaiah, which has been well answered by conservative scholarship. Therefore we will not waste time by delving into it. I find it interesting that Jeremiah quoted from Micah, which reveals the importance of Micah in his day. "Micah the Morasthite prophesied in the days of Hezekiah king of Judah, and spake to all the people of Judah, saying, thus saith the LORD of hosts; Zion shall be plowed like a field, and Jerusalem shall become heaps, and the mountain of the house as the high places of a forest" (Jer. 26:18). Of course, the people paid no more attention to Jeremiah than they had to Micah, and what Micah had prophesied did happen to Jerusalem exactly as he said it would.

Many folk, especially young preachers who want to give an exposition, have asked me how to begin. I would say, not only to young preachers but to everyone who wants to study the Bible, first of all, get a grasp of the message of an entire book. What is it all about? What is the author trying to say? What is the main message? To get this information you must outline the book. In Micah we find that the message is, "Who is like God in proclaiming, in prophesying, in pleading, and in pardoning?" That is how the Book of Micah is divided.

OUTLINE

"WHO IS A GOD LIKE UNTO THEE?"

I. **Proclaiming Future Judgment for Past Sins, Chapters 1—3**
   - A. Prophet's First Message Directed Against Samaria, Reaches to Jerusalem, Chapter 1
   - B. Prophet's Second Message Describes Specific Sins, Chapter 2
   - C. Prophet's Third Message Denounces Leaders for Sins, Chapter 3

II. **Prophesying Future Glory Because of Past Promises, Chapters 4—5**
   - A. Prophecies of Last Days, Chapter 4
   - B. Prophecy of First Coming of Christ Before Second Coming and Kingdom, Chapter 5

III. **Pleading Present Repentance Because of Past Redemption, Chapter 6**

IV. **Pardoning All Iniquity Because of Who God Is and What He Does, Chapter 7**

CHAPTER 1

THEME: The prophet's first message, directed against
Samaria, reaches to Jerusalem

The first three chapters, as I have indicated in the Introduction, are
denunciatory.

In every chapter of this remarkable little book there will be a striking statement—sometimes in a single verse, sometimes in many
verses as in this first chapter.

**The word of the LORD that came to Micah the Morasthite
in the days of Jotham, Ahaz, and Hezekiah, kings of Judah, which he saw concerning Samaria and Jerusalem
[Mic. 1:1].**

Let me repeat, Samaria was the capital of the northern kingdom. The
city was built originally by Omri, king of Israel, and was the seat of
idolatry. It was made famous—or infamous—by Ahab and Jezebel who
built there a temple to Baal. The city stood in a very lovely location,
but it lies in ruins today. I have pictures of it, which I took while on a
trip to Israel. The desolate ruins bear mute testimony to the accuracy
of Micah's prophecy concerning Samaria.

"Micah the Morasthite" means that he was a native of Moresheth
of Gath, which is southwest of Jerusalem. Although he was in the
kingdom of Judah, he prophesied to both kingdoms, but his main
message was directed to the northern kingdom. I have often wondered
about that. His contemporary, Isaiah, was a prophet to the southern
kingdom; and perhaps, since Micah was probably a younger man, he
felt that Isaiah could take care of the southern kingdom while God
directed him to speak to the northern kingdom. You will never misunderstand Micah, because he makes it very clear to whom he is speaking.

THE PROPHET'S FIRST MESSAGE

Hear, all ye people; hearken, O earth, and all that therein is: and let the Lord GOD be witness against you, the Lord from his holy temple [Mic. 1:2].

"Hear, all ye people" means *all* people. That includes you wherever you are today. Micah has a message for us. As with all the prophets, although speaking into a particular situation which has long since disappeared, his message is relevant for our day because certain principles are laid down. Micah gives a philosophy of human government. He deals with that which is false and that which is true authority in government. This would be a good book for both Republicans and Democrats in Washington to consider. It wouldn't hurt them to look at *God's* philosophy of government because, very candidly, their form of government is not working today. The reason it cannot work properly is because it was originally put together by men who, although some of them were not Christians, had a respect and reverence for the Bible. They felt that the great principles stated in the Bible were worth following, and therefore they wove them into the warp and woof of our government. It will never work in the hands of godless men. Frankly, that is our problem. Actually, the *form* of government is not the important feature, although we think it is. Let me give you an example: when Cromwell was a dictator in England, they had about the best form of government they could possibly have had. Don't misunderstand me, I am not recommending a dictatorship, but it is good if you have the right dictator. When Jesus comes to reign on this earth, my friend, *He* is going to be a dictator and the right kind of dictator. The character of the ruler is of utmost importance. It makes no difference if there is a monarchy, a limited monarchy, an autocracy, a democracy, or a representative form of government; if the right men are in charge, it will work. I hope that I am getting it over to you that I am not talking politics, but I am speaking of a philosophy of government and am attempting to pinpoint our current problem. We need men in government who have *character*. The concern of the American people is whether or not their government leaders have TV personalities. We are more interested in charisma than character. Micah deals with this matter in the third chapter: "The heads thereof judge for reward, and the priests thereof teach for hire, and the prophets thereof divine for money: yet will they lean upon the LORD, and say, Is not the LORD among us? none evil can come upon us" (Mic. 3:11). Micah puts his finger on the fact that they had *false* prophets, false religion, and false leaders.

"Hearken, O earth, and all that therein is." Since most of us are on this earth, he means all of us.

"And let the Lord GOD be witness against you." Micah is calling God as a witness to the thing which he is going to say.

"The Lord from his holy temple." The Lord was in His holy temple, in His heaven, then as now.

The Lord will come down in judgment—

> For, behold, the LORD cometh forth out of his place, and will come down, and tread upon the high places of the earth [Mic. 1:3].

This language is absolutely beautiful, although it is frightful in many ways.

"Tread upon the high places of the earth." You recall that the high places were the locations of idol worship. Idols were set up in groves upon the hills and mountains. Also in that day the cities were situated on elevated places. Both Samaria and Jerusalem were built on mountains. The Lord Jesus mentioned that a city that is set upon a hill cannot be hid, and the city has a tremendous influence upon the area around it (see Matt. 5:14). When the city is the seat of government, it has a tremendous influence not only upon the immediate area but often upon the entire world. That is the case of many great cities in the past and present. Also cities are centers of great sin. For these reasons God is coming down upon them in judgment—He will "tread upon the high places of the earth."

> And the mountains shall be molten under him, and the valleys shall be cleft, as wax before the fire, and as the waters that are poured down a steep place [Mic. 1:4].

"The mountains shall be molten [melted] under him, and the valleys shall be cleft." This is definitely a picture of volcanic action and of earthquakes. We find this same language in the Scriptures from Judges through Habakkuk. For example, Psalm 18:7–10: "Then the earth shook and trembled; the foundations also of the hills moved and were shaken, because he was wroth. There went up a smoke out of his nostrils, and fire out of his mouth devoured: coals were kindled by it. He bowed the heavens also, and came down: and darkness was under his feet. And he rode upon a cherub, and did fly: yea, he did fly upon the wings of the wind." Although this language is highly figurative, it is a tremendous, actual, exact picture of what took place.

This raises a question about what or who controls the weather and natural forces. Well, God is the One who controls nature and earthquakes and volcanoes and weather. I believe that God judges nations and that He judges peoples, and these things are warnings. I have always felt the Great Depression of the 1930s and the dust storms in the Midwest were warnings from God. But America didn't listen to God. Then we entered World War II, and we have not recovered from that yet. God is still moving in the affairs of this world.

I think of Turkey, especially along the west coast, and the ruins of the great cities like Ephesus and Pergamos which at one time were the very lifeblood of the Roman Empire. Now they are lying in ruins. Why is it that there is no great population but only little towns there today? Well, you may say, it is earthquake territory. You are right. It is interesting that man always flocks to earthquake territory. That is true in California where I live. I have seen people come out here by the millions. We are ready for an earthquake, let me tell you. The greatest population of the Roman Empire was in modern Turkey, and look what happened to it. Historians tell us that an earthquake destroyed the cities and caused the people to flee. That was the judgment of God, you see.

God makes it clear here about His judgment—

For the transgression of Jacob is all this, and for the sins of the house of Israel. What is the transgression of Ja-

cob? is it not Samaria? and what are the high places of Judah? are they not Jerusalem? [Mic. 1:5].

"For the transgression of Jacob . . . and for the sins of the house of Israel." You see, he is speaking to both kingdoms and their capitals— Samaria of Israel and Jerusalem of Judah (or Jacob).

"What is the transgression of Jacob?" Rather, *who* is responsible for the transgression of Jacob? The answer is: "Is it not Samaria? and what are the high places of Judah? are they not Jerusalem?" The prophet places the blame on the capital cities, Jerusalem and Samaria. Jerusalem was the place where they were to worship God. Were they worshiping Him there? Well, yes, they would go to the temple, but they also were going to the high places where idolatry and the grossest forms of immorality took place. And God says that it is for these things He is going to judge these two great cities because of their tremendous influence over the nations of Israel and Judah.

This has, I believe, an application to my own nation because we have a philosophy of government that is wrong. As we have seen, it is not the *form* of government that is wrong; it is the *people* who head it up who are wrong. I do not know that there is too much difference between having one godless dictator or having a whole godless Senate and a whole godless House of Representatives. The founders of our nation formed three branches of government because they had had a bad experience with old King George back in England, and they knew they could not trust men. Their theory was that the three branches of government could watch each other. Well, in our day all three need watching. Why? Because it takes the right kind of men for any government to function properly.

The problem in Micah's day was that Samaria and Jerusalem had become corrupt, and God was going to judge them. What about my own country? It is my personal opinion that America has gone over the hill. The United States does not appear in the prophecies of the end times for one of two reasons: either it will have disappeared as a nation or it will no longer be a world power. We had a marvelous opportunity to lead the world following World War II. So what did we give the world? We gave it rock music, hippies, the new morality, a love of pleasure, and a love of affluence. And today the United States of America is on the way down. This is distressing to me because I *love* my country, and I hate to see a godless outfit take over and spoil this nation which I do believe was founded under God for a very definite purpose. It is a government *under God* that Micah is espousing. This is God's philosophy of government, you see.

Now we come to the first striking statement, and it is the longest one. It goes through the remainder of the chapter, from verse 6 to verse 16. It is a miniature of the great destruction that will come in the last days. We will return to the subject of judgment during the last days when we come to the fourth chapter of Micah; but, here in the first chapter of Micah, it is a local judgment in which Assyria will destroy Samaria. I wish I could show you some of my pictures of Samaria. At one time it was a lovely city. It was a city of great influence and culture. It was a city of great promise, but today it lies in dust and ashes.

Therefore I will make Samaria as an heap of the field, and as plantings of a vineyard: and I will pour down the stones thereof into the valley, and I will discover the foundations thereof [Mic. 1:6].

"I will make Samaria as an heap of the field, and as plantings of a vineyard." That is what it is today. I saw a little vineyard planted by Arabs growing right in the ruins of one section of Samaria. There are other places where you can find an orchard planted in the ruins and different kinds of trees which were planted here and there.

"I will pour down the stones thereof into the valley." I have stood on the acropolis, the very highest place in Samaria, and have looked down the steep embankment. Do you know what is down there? There are all kinds of pillars and stones that formerly had been hewn out and used in buildings. They have been rolled down, down into the valley. I can't think of anything more literal than this fulfillment of "I will pour down the stones thereof into the valley."

"And I will discover [uncover] the foundations thereof." I would like to show you the pictures I took of the foundations which were there in the time of Ahab and Jezebel. Also I have pictures of the later foundations which were built by the Romans. God has uncovered them all, and they are all there in ruins for you to take a good look at today. The foundations reveal that there had been a tremendous city there, but it has long since gone out of business.

> **And all the graven images thereof shall be beaten to pieces, and all the hires thereof shall be burned with the fire, and all the idols thereof will I lay desolate: for she gathered it of the hire of an harlot, and they shall return to the hire of an harlot [Mic. 1:7].**

"And all the graven [carved] images thereof shall be beaten to pieces." When I was there, I asked my guide, "Are there any images around here? Have the archaeologists found any images?" His answer was, "No. There is no evidence of idolatry although we know that there was idolatry here." Let me remind you that the high places which are mentioned were places where idols stood and where the basest kind of worship took place. For example, in the worship of Molech, the idol formed a red-hot oven where children were actually offered. What an awful thing that was! And the grossest forms of immorality were carried on in connection with idol worship. In other words, religion and illicit sex were very much the same thing. It is abroad again today in Satan worship and outgrowths of the occult.

"And all the hires thereof shall be burned with the fire." The word *hires* is very interesting. It refers to the costly vessels that had been given to the heathen temples. My guide told me that, in the ruins of the palace of Jezebel, archaeologists have found remains of quite a few smaller ivory vessels which were evidently jars to hold perfume and some larger ones to hold wine. There has been a great deal of excavation done there.

"She gathered it of the hire of an harlot, and they shall return to the hire of an harlot." Sex was at the heart of these idolatrous rites. In Corinth, for instance, they know today that in the worship of Aphrodite upon the Acropolis, there were a thousand "vestal virgins," who were nothing in the world but prostitutes. Sex was a part of the religion. A man had to *pay* when he went into one of their places of worship. Whether in temples or out-of-doors, they were brothels. It was all done in the name of religion. This was true among the Phoenicians; it was true among the Philistines; and Israel had adopted their religions.

It is quite interesting that contemporary thought is returning to that viewpoint. The so-called "new morality" is as old as the worship of Molech and of Baal and of other heathen religions of antiquity. This is one reason I insist that religion has not been a blessing to the world. If you want to see what religion has done, go to India. There religion has kept a wonderful people in a pitiful state. The people are absolutely impoverished and *bound* by the fetters of religion. Christianity, of course, is not a religion; Christianity is a Person. The Lord Jesus made that clear when He said, "If the Son therefore shall make you free, ye shall be free indeed" (John 8:36). He can deliver you from things that are sinful, and He can also deliver you from the bondage of religion.

The last part of the verse says, "she gathered it of the hire of an harlot, and they shall return to the hire of an harlot." Micah is saying that the hires will go right back and be used for sin again. Some of these vessels were apparently used again in Roman times. It was Herod who rebuilt that city. He liked the location; it was a delightful place to live, but it also has been destroyed and is in ruins today. Heathen worship was the main sin. It was number one on the sin parade, but Micah is going to mention some other sins, too.

LAMENTATION OF MICAH

The remainder of the chapter is Micah's lamentation. He is deeply affected by Israel's sins and their consequences. Micah is not just a paid preacher; he is a prophet called of God. He is very much like Jeremiah and Hosea in that he had a tender heart. We tend to think of all the Old Testament prophets as being hard-nosed like Elijah and Ezekiel. You may remember that, when God commissioned Ezekiel, He warned that He was sending him to an impudent and hardhearted people. But, He said, "I am going to make your head harder than theirs." There was a need for hardheaded prophets, and these men could speak right out; but many of God's prophets were very tender-hearted, and Micah was one of them. Listen to him—

Therefore I will wail and howl, I will go stripped and naked: I will make a wailing like the dragons, and mourning as the owls [Mic. 1:8].

"I will go stripped and naked." When a man removed his outer garments, it meant that he was in deep mourning and deep trouble.

"I will make a wailing like the dragons [jackals], and mourning as the owls [ostriches]." If you have ever heard a wolf or a hyena howl at night, you know it is a mournful and terrible sound. Job uses this same expression: "I am a brother to dragons [jackals], and a companion to owls [ostriches]" (Job 30:29). I did not know that ostriches mourn until several years ago when my wife and I were visiting the San Diego Zoo. We were walking around when we heard a mournful sound. It was a very plaintive and pitiful sort of a sound. At first I thought an animal had been trapped or hurt in some way. As we continued our walk, we met a man and I asked him, "Do you know what is making that sound?" He replied, "It's the ostriches." I thought the man was pulling my leg. I didn't even thank him for the information because I thought he was kidding. But soon we walked around a bend in the road, and there were the ostriches. They were all standing there, just looking around. I didn't see any reason for their mourning, but they were making the most mournful sound I have ever heard. Micah said that he would mourn like the ostriches. He would wail like they did.

In other words, the message that this man was giving to the people was affecting him just as the message that Jeremiah gave affected him. This is another example of the type of man God wants to deliver a harsh message. It must be a man with a tender heart if the message is to be harsh. Why? Because before God judges a people, He wants them to know how *He* feels; so He sent the weeping prophet Jeremiah and then this weeping prophet Micah. When the people listen to his message, then to his mourning and wailing, they understand how God feels about their sin. God is not vindictive. Although He takes no delight in judgment, He must judge sin. If you will turn that over in your mind a little, my friend, you will recognize that God cannot permit evil and wrong to be done to one of His creatures without His judging the guilty party. He would not be God if He did not give justice to His creatures. When evil is done and sin is committed, God is going to move in judgment. It takes Him a little while to get around to it; but, when He moves, nothing can stop Him.

> **For her wound is incurable; for it is come unto Judah; he**
> **is come unto the gate of my people, even to Jerusalem**
> **[Mic. 1:9].**

"Her wound is incurable." The nation had passed over an invisible line from which there was no possibility of returning. While I do not know where that line is, I do know it exists. And when an individual or a nation passes over that line, there is no possibility of reclamation. It is not that God is not merciful and gracious, but the individual or the nation is so bent to sin and has turned a deaf ear to God for so long that there is nothing left but judgment. The wound is incurable. They will no longer hear God.

This disturbs me, because I wonder if my own country may have passed over that line. All I know is that they are not hearing the voice of God and do not want to hear it. In spite of the fact that there is a tremendous reception today for the Word of God, I sometimes wonder how deep it is. Are the *hearing* of the Word of God and *obedience* to the Word of God synonymous? I actually know of folk who are living in sin or have lived in sin and never repented of it, yet speak of *loving* the Word of God! Is it possible that they have stepped over that invisible line and that there is nothing left for them but judgment?

"For her wound is incurable; for it is come unto Judah; he is come unto the gate of my people, even to Jerusalem." The Assyrian army under Sennacherib came down from the north and mowed down the northern kingdom. They got as far south as the walls of Jerusalem, and the king Hezekiah was afraid that they were going to take the city; but

God instructed Isaiah to tell the king that Jerusalem would not be invaded but that this was a warning to them. Well, Judah heeded the warning for awhile, but it wore off and they turned back to their idol worship and their sin. The day came when God had to judge Judah as He had judged Israel.

Now we are given a series of names of ten different urban centers that were affected by Samaria and Jerusalem. Not all of these places are on the map, but the list begins in the north with Samaria and moves south toward Jerusalem and beyond Jerusalem. The meanings of the names reveal a play upon words.

> **Declare ye it not at Gath, weep ye not at all: in the house of Aphrah roll thyself in the dust [Mic. 1:10].**

"Declare ye it not at Gath." The name *Gath* means "weep-town." God is saying, "Weep not at Weep-town." Gath belonged to the Philistines, the inveterate enemies of Israel, and He is saying, "Don't let them know that judgment is coming upon you."

"In the house of Aphrah roll thyself in the dust." *Aphrah* means "dust-town." To put dust on the head was the sign of the deepest grief. The site of this town is not known, but the thought seems to be that the people were to lament in their own territory.

> **Pass ye away, thou inhabitant of Saphir, having thy shame naked: the inhabitant of Zaanan came not forth in the mourning of Beth-ezel; he shall receive of you his standing [Mic. 1:11].**

Saphir means "beauty-town." Believe me, the inhabitants passed away and also the town itself so that the site of it is absolutely unknown. Beauty-town would be no longer beautiful—"having thy shame naked."

"The inhabitant of Zaanan came not forth in the mourning." *Zaanan* means "march-town." March-town didn't march. The site of this town is also unknown to us.

For the inhabitant of Maroth waited carefully for good: but evil came down from the LORD unto the gate of Jerusalem [Mic. 1:12].

"The inhabitant of Maroth waited carefully [anxiously] for good." The name *Maroth* means "bitterness." They waited for a good report, for good news, but it was a bitter report—"evil came down from the LORD unto the age of Jerusalem." The Assyrians were marching to the very walls of Jerusalem.

O thou inhabitant of Lachish, bind the chariot to the swift beast: she is the beginning of the sin to the daughter of Zion: for the transgressions of Israel were found in thee [Mic. 1:13].

Lachish was "Horse-town." There were great stables of horses there. It is a city southwest of Jerusalem, over near the Philistine country, the place where idolatry was first introduced into the southern kingdom of Judah. Apparently Lachish was the link of idolatry between Israel and Judah.

"Bind the chariot to the swift beast" is a reference to the horse, and we know know that this is the place where horses were kept which were used in the worship of the sun. You will recall that even the Greeks had their Apollo driving a chariot across the sky in connection with their worship of the sun. God is condemning Lachish because she introduced this idolatry into Judah, the southern kingdom.

Therefore shalt thou give presents to Moresheth-gath: the houses of Achzib shall be a lie to the kings of Israel [Mic. 1:14].

"Moresheth-gath" was, of course, the hometown of Micah; it was in the southern kingdom of Judah.

"The houses of Achzib shall be a lie to the kings of Israel." *Achzib* means "lie-town." Lie-town, as did all these other towns, lived up to its name. The inhabitants were given over to lies. The name *Achzib* is the Hebrew word for a "winter brook" or a "lie." The reason for this is that the brooks in Israel are very much like the brooks in Southern California. In fact, a friend of mine was riding with me one day when we crossed over the Los Angeles River. In the winter, during the wet season, this river can really go on a rampage, but in the dry season there is not much more than a trickle of water in it. As we crossed the river, my friend said, "That's a good place for a river." I replied, "It sure is, and in the winter there is a river there." In Israel there are many dry river beds like that. But a flash flood out in the desert can transform them into raging torrents. Now you can see why *achzib* means a "winter brook" or a "lie." And the town of Achzib was Lie-town because they had promised help to the northern kingdom, but they actually gave no help at all. "The houses of Achzib shall be a lie to the kings of Israel."

> **Yet will I bring an heir unto thee, O inhabitant of Mareshah: he shall come unto Adullam the glory of Israel [Mic. 1:15].**

Here is a suggestion that help is coming to Israel but not at this time. It is only a faint suggestion that "the glory of Israel" is the heir in the line of David, and the Lord Jesus Christ is the only one who fits this description. One of His names is *Faithful*—He is faithful and true, and He *is* coming to deliver them. He will not come from Lie-town, that's for sure. However, in Micah's day Israel was deceived, greatly deceived, and no help came to them when the Assyrian army came down from the north and overran their land.

Now Micah calls upon Israel to mourn as a nation—

> **Make thee bald, and poll thee for thy delicate children; enlarge thy baldness as the eagle; for they are gone into captivity from thee [Mic. 1:16].**

When Assyria invaded Israel the first time, they took the young people into captivity, and the people are called upon to mourn because of that. Making themselves bald was an indication of grief. Although in the Mosaic Law they were told not to trim their beards nor shave their beards, now because of the sin that had come into the nation they are told to express their grief in this manner.

Isaiah, who was a contemporary of Micah, had something to say about this custom. In Isaiah 15:2 we read, "He is gone up to Bajith, and to Dibon, the high places [of idolatry], to weep: Moab shall howl over Nebo, and over Medeba: on all their heads shall be baldness, and every beard cut off." This verse describes deep mourning and wailing. They had lost their children, you see. This is the judgment of God upon them.

CHAPTER 2

THEME: The prophet's second message describes specific sins

THE PROPHET'S SECOND MESSAGE

In this chapter Micah describes the specific sins of the people. Judgment came upon these people because they had gone into idolatry with all that that implies. Idolatry in that day represented gross immorality, and the wages of the harlots ran the "high places." Prostitution was the source of funds for their religion since sex was associated with idolatry. We find that the same thing is true today in the occult and in Satan worship. I think there is a connection between the occult of today and the idolatry of Micah's day. Sex plays a very prominent part in both of them. They are a revelation of man breaking God's commandment. Sexual sin and idolatry seem to go together. They destroy the home and destroy the sweet and tender relationship between a man and a woman in marriage. When sex is kept within the marriage relationship, it can become the sweetest and most precious thing on earth. When a nation moves sex out of that context and encourages illicit sex in the name of religion or "new morality," it is evidence of the fact that the nation is in decline and is actually on its way out.

The sins which Micah will denounce in this chapter are sins against one another, sins against mankind, while in the first chapter their sins were in their relationship with God. You see, when a man is not right with God, he cannot be right with his fellowman. And when a man is right with God, he can be (although he doesn't always choose to be) right with his fellowman. We have an illustration of this in the lovey-dovey movement which started several years ago with the "flower children" in the San Francisco area. Because they were far from the Lord, the movement lapsed into gross immorality, and it wrecked the lives of many young people. My friend, when you are not right with God, you will not be right with other people.

Chapter 2 is not going to be pretty. You will not find it to be the most beautiful chapter in the Word of God. But it reveals the sin of a nation, which caused its destruction. It is well for us as God's people and also for our nation to listen to Micah and to wake up.

Woe to them that devise iniquity, and work evil upon their beds! when the morning is light, they practise it, because it is in the power of their hand [Mic. 2:1].

Although this may include the practice of illicit sex, it primarily refers to evil of other sorts. When they go to bed at night, they don't go to sleep but lie there and devise and plan iniquity—and chances are they are engaging in it at the same time. I have had some experience with folk like this. A wife complained to me bitterly that when her husband comes home, he doesn't leave his work in the office but brings it with him. And when he goes to bed at night, he lies there conniving what he will do the next day. No wonder the wife was contemplating divorce.

"When the morning is light, they practise it, because it is in the power of their hand." That is, they are able to execute what they have planned. It is also true in our contemporary society that the sinner and the ungodly are successful. The wealth of my own country is not in the hands of the godly today—although it was at one time. Money means power, and the ungodly are able to carry through that which is wrong. This is the chief reason that my nation is in its present predicament. The real problem is not an energy shortage nor the incapability of this or that political party. The root of the problem is that power is in the hands of the ungodly. This is the same sin which brought Israel down. Micah, as we have already noted, presents a philosophy of human government which God follows. If you doubt this, read the history of the fall of great nations. When wealth and power get into the hands of a few ungodly people, God moves in judgment.

Micah is still speaking of those in his day whose lives were characterized by doing evil—twenty-four hours a day. Now he is being specific—

And they covet fields, and take them by violence; and houses, and take them away: so they oppress a man and his house, even a man and his heritage [Mic. 2:2].

"They covet fields, and take them by violence." We have an example of this being done by Israel's royalty in the case of Ahab and Jezebel. In 1 Kings 21 we have the record of King Ahab coveting the vineyard of Naboth. Like a spoiled brat, he wanted it, although he didn't make a move to get it. However, his wife Jezebel was a sinner who believed in action. She immediately set about getting the vineyard by eliminating Naboth. So what the heads of government practiced, those down below began to practice. The wealthy began to seize the fields that they coveted because they had the money and the power to do it.

My, how that method is being used in our contemporary society! The little businessman doesn't stand much of a chance for survival in the culture we have produced. The big operators are in control, and they frankly say that they are in for the profits. But sometimes the word *profit* is a synonym for *covetousness*. And this was the great sin of Israel.

I have never understood why any man would want more than one million dollars. I have always thought that if I had that much money I would never want any more. It seems, however, that when a man gets one million dollars, he desires two million dollars. With two million dollars he can't eat any more. He can't sleep any more. He can't indulge himself any more—he can only drink so much, and he can only sin so much. A million dollars will enable a man to do all that he wants, but men want to continue to get richer and richer and richer. The old bromide "The rich get richer and the poor get poorer" is the story of mankind. And Micah is speaking into that situation.

Notice that evil men will covet fields and houses and take them by violence. God not only gave the Land of Promise to the nation Israel and put them in it, but He also gave each tribe a particular portion of the land. Then He gave each individual a particular plot in the tribe to which he belonged, and that plot was his heritage. Then God instituted certain laws so that a man could not lose his land forever. During the Year of Jubilee every mortgage was canceled, and every bit of property was returned to its original owner. However, the Year of Jubilee only came every fifty years. If you lost your land the second year after Jubilee, you would have to wait forty-eight years to reclaim it. You could get very hungry in that length of time! Even though God had made laws to protect the poor, the rich always found ways to get around them, of course. All through the Scriptures we see that God is on the side of the poor. As Abraham Lincoln used to say, "God must love poor people because He made so many of them." And the Lord Jesus Himself experienced the poverty of this earth.

> **Therefore thus saith the LORD; Behold, against this family do I devise an evil, from which ye shall not remove your necks; neither shall ye go haughtily: for this time is evil [Mic. 2:3].**

This is a very interesting verse. God has said, "I condemn you because you lie on your beds and plot evil." Now He says, "I am going to plot evil against you." What does He mean by that? Was God actually going to do that which was evil? No, God intended to punish the evildoers, which was right, but from their viewpoint it was wrong because they wouldn't like that. They would call it evil.

Today even some Christians condemn God for permitting certain things to take place. In other words, they are saying that God is doing evil. Well, God beat them to it; He said that He would do evil from their viewpoint. If they continued sinning, he would stop them with judgment. In fact, He said to Israel, "I devise an evil, from which ye shall not remove your necks." God intended to put around those necks the chains of bondage. And the people of Israel were led captive into Assyria, one of the most brutal nations that has ever been on the topside of this earth. God adds, "Neither shall ye go haughtily: for this time is evil." How haughty and proud they had been!

My own nation is presently in this same position. In many countries that I have visited—South America, Europe, Africa, and Asia—I have found that Americans are not loved, and we haven't been loved for many years. Why? Because we have been haughty and proud. Yet we had the temerity after World War II to tell the world that we were going to lead it to peace! We thought the American dollar would solve the problems of the world. Well, we have gotten this world into a mess, haven't we? And American diplomacy has been nothing to boast about since World War II. Why has our record been so poor? My personal opinion is that the judgment of God is already taking place. I love my country, and it breaks my heart to see it continue to fall into the hands of the godless rich. Let me repeat that it is not the *method* of government but the character of the men who govern that makes a nation great.

> In that day shall one take up a parable against you, and lament with a doleful lamentation, and say, We be utterly spoiled: he hath changed the portion of my people: how hath he removed it from me! turning away he hath divided our fields [Mic. 2:4].

Great confusion was coming and "doleful lamentation"—a very unusual expression in the Hebrew language. It probably would not be possible to translate into English exactly what Micah was saying. There was no hope at all—"We be utterly spoiled [destroyed]."

> Therefore thou shalt have none that shall cast a cord by lot in the congregation of the LORD [Mic. 2:5].

There have been various interpretations of this. Perhaps it means that there will be no more worship of God in that place.

> Prophesy ye not, say they to them that prophesy: they shall not prophesy to them, that they shall not take shame.
>
> O thou that art named the house of Jacob, is the spirit of the LORD straitened? are these his doings? do not my words do good to him that walketh uprightly? [Mic. 2:6-7].

This was a time when God cut off the flow of the spirit of prophecy. Why? Because the people wouldn't hear it, and there came a famine of the Word of God.

"Are these his doings?" God has told them that He, too, is plotting evil—that is, what *they* call evil, because it is going to be a judgment against them.

"Do not my words do good to him that walketh uprightly?" Though the message is harsh, God's people will accept it, and they will obey it. This is not a delightful passage like Psalm 23 or John 14, but God gives it just as much prominence. In fact, He put it in the second chapter, rather than in the fourteenth or the twenty-third, so we would not miss it.

Even of late my people is risen up as an enemy: ye pull off the robe with the garment from them that pass by securely as men averse from war [Mic. 2:8].

God is saying that, although they are His people, they have become His enemies, and one of the evidences of this is the way they treat the poor. God always insists upon justice for the poor. His charge is: "Ye pull off the robe with the garment from them." A man's robe was what he slept in. In other words, they would take a man's bed out from under him. That was how far they were willing to go to rob the poor.

The women of my people have ye cast out from their pleasant houses; from their children have ye taken away my glory for ever [Mic. 2:9].

"The women of my people have ye cast out from their pleasant houses" probably refers to unprotected widows who had inherited homes from their husbands.

"From their children have ye taken away my glory for ever." Even the young children were deprived of what God had given to them. And they would grow up in rebellion. In our day the rebellion of youth is, in my opinion, permitted by God to try to shake us out of our lethargy.

> Arise ye, and depart; for this is not your rest: because it
> is polluted, it shall destroy you, even with a sore de-
> struction [Mic. 2:10].

They were attempting to solve their problems and to be at rest without
being at peace with God. "Because it is polluted, it shall destroy you
even with a sore [great] destruction." Because of the pollution of their
sin and their heartless oppression, the land would cast out its inhabitants.

> If a man walking in the spirit and falsehood do lie, say-
> ing, I will prophesy unto thee of wine and of strong
> drink; he shall even be the prophet of this people [Mic.
> 2:11].

This is biting sarcasm. God is saying, "The kind of prophets you want
are those who will approve of your sins." My friend, in our day many
people do not want the preacher to say that drinking is wrong and that
drunkenness is bad. Even in our churches many pastors are approv-
ing of social drinking. They insist that we are living in a new day, and,
since we are not under the Mosaic Law, we can do these things. While
it is true that we are under grace, there is one sure thing: if you love
God, you are going to go keep His commandments, and He certainly
does condemn drunkenness. The false prophets in Micah's day were
not condemning the sins of the people. They were popular preachers,
saying what the people wanted to hear.

PROMISE TO THE REMNANT

The message of judgment which Micah has been delivering has been
very harsh, but here at the close of the chapter is a very beautiful little
prophecy which shines like a ray of sunshine that breaks through the
dark clouds of a stormy day.

> I will surely assemble, O Jacob, all of thee; I will surely
> gather the remnant of Israel; I will put them together as

the sheep of Bozrah, as the flock in the midst of their fold: they shall make great noise by reason of the multitude of men [Mic. 2:12].

You have noticed, I am sure, that when God speaks to them of their sin, He addresses them by the name *Jacob*. So when He uses that term in this verse, the implication is that He is going to show mercy to them, not because of their worthiness or because of some fine character trait, but because of His own grace.

"I will surely assemble, O Jacob, all of thee." This was not fulfilled after the Babylonian captivity, and it has not been fulfilled in their recent return to their land because He says that He will assemble "*all*" of thee." At the present time, there are more of the nation Israel in New York City than there are in the whole land of Israel. Also, there is a great company still in Russia and in other countries of the world. So God has not yet assembled all of them according to this prophecy.

"I will surely gather the remnant of Israel." Now for the remnant He uses the name Israel. God has always had a faithful remnant out of the nation, and actually He has never had more than the remnant. There never has been a time when it could be said that 100 percent of the nation had turned to God. And it was always for the sake of the remnant that God was gracious to the nation. In the future day that is coming, even in the Great Tribulation period when we are told that all Israel shall be saved, who is meant? Well, it is all of Israel which belongs to that company of 144,000. The Book of Revelation makes it clear that they will be sealed (sealed, I believe, by the Holy Spirit of God) and will be able to survive the Great Tribulation. But that will be only a remnant of the nation. After all, there are probably three million Jews in Israel and probably twelve million in other lands, so that 144,000 could be nothing more than a remnant.

"I will put them together as the sheep of Bozrah." Bozrah was a place of many flocks of sheep because of the excellent pasture lands. When God brings His people together like the sheep of Bozrah, the Twenty-third Psalm will be fulfilled: "The LORD is my shepherd; I shall not want. He maketh me to lie down in green pastures . . ." (Ps. 23:1–2).

"They shall make great noise by reason of the multitude of men."
The great noise will be due to the fact that a great number will return
to the land. When God returns the nation to their land, it does not
mean that all of them are going to be saved by any means; but it will be
a tremendous event. Since what *we* have seen of the return of Israel to
the land has caused such great rejoicing among prophetic teachers,
think what it will be in this future day!

> **The breaker is come up before them: they have broken
> up, and have passed through the gate, and are gone out
> by it: and their king shall pass before them, and the
> LORD on the head of them [Mic. 2:13].**

"The breaker is come up before them." The "breaker" is the one who
clears the way, removes the obstacles, and leads them. I believe this
refers to their entering the millennial Kingdom when the Lord Jesus
Christ will be the one to lead them, as He will have returned to the
earth at that time. This verse refers to Him as the Breaker, their King,
and the Lord (Jehovah).

CHAPTER 3

THEME: The prophet's third message denouces leaders
for their sins

THE PROPHET'S THIRD MESSAGE

Micah denounces the leaders of Israel for their sins—first, the princes; second, the prophets, who were the spiritual leaders; and last, all the leaders of Jerusalem, including the princes, the prophets, and the priests.

SINS OF THE PRINCES

This section begins with the call to hear, as does every major division of the Book of Micah.

> **And I said, Hear, I pray you, O heads of Jacob, and ye princes of the house of Israel; Is it not for you to know judgment? [Mic. 3:1].**

"Hear, I pray you, O heads of Jacob." He is speaking to the leadership of the nation.

"Is it not for you to know judgment?" What does he mean by this? Well, he is addressing the rulers of Israel who were the judges and magistrates. When the people were found guilty of a crime, they were brought before these men for judgment. Now *they* certainly should know what judgment and justice are. The same thought is expressed in the New Testament: "Therefore thou art inexcusable, O man, whosoever thou art that judgest: for wherein thou judgest another, thou condemnest thyself; for thou that judgest doest the same things" (Rom. 2:1). "The same things" does not mean *identical* but *similar* things. An example of this is found in 2 Samuel 12. The prophet Nathan came before King David and told him about a rich man in his kingdom who had great flocks of sheep. However, when he needed

MICAH 3   109

meat to serve his guest, instead of taking a lamb from his own flock, he took a poor man's little ewe lamb—the only lamb he owned—and roasted it for his guest. When David heard this, he stood up, hot with anger, and pronounced judgment upon the man who would do such a thing. He could see the injustice of it; yet he himself had done a similar thing. And Nathan said to David, ". . . Thou art the man . . ." (2 Sam. 12:7). David accepted the judgment and confessed his guilt before God. It is amazing, friend, how we can see another man's sin but overlook our own. This is the reason God says to these leaders in Israel, "You have judged others for their misdeeds, but you are doing the same things."

This charge is certainly applicable to our day also. My feeling is that the reason many judges in our land have been so lenient with criminals and have not wanted the death penalty is that they are bothered by a guilt complex themselves. I have a notion that many times when a judge on the bench hears a case of an offender who is brought before him and hands down a light sentence, it is because it salves his own conscience to do so. It is almost a joke when a group of congressmen investigate the wrongdoing of someone in politics. Probably every one of them sitting there judging the other fellow has a skeleton in his own closet. It takes men of character to judge fairly, you see.

This is exactly what Micah is saying to the leadership in his day, "Is it not for you to know judgment?" You are not acting in ignorance; you have had experience in this. You have judged men who were guilty; now you are guilty.

Who hate the good, and love the evil; who pluck off their skin from off them, and their flesh from off their bones [Mic. 3:2].

"Who hate the good, and love the evil." It is difficult for a judge who had been at a cocktail party the night before and had become a little tipsy himself to sentence a man the next day who has killed somebody because he was driving while drunk. No wonder the judge lets him off easy. I know what I am talking about, my friend, because my mother was killed by a drunken driver right here in Pasadena. I didn't feel that I should press charges, but when I was called in as a witness, I told the court, "All I ask is that justice be done." And, believe me, he got off with a light sentence. As I looked at that judge, I had the feeling that he had a pretty bad conscience.

In Micah's day the leadership actually hated the good and loved the evil. Folk like that are not fit to be in positions of leadership then or now. If it is discovered that a man in a high position in government—a congressman, a senator, or a judge—is unfaithful to his wife, is he fit to make laws relative to marriage? I don't think so. The present breakdown in morality goes back to the lawmakers. And God puts the blame on the leadership of the nation Israel in Micah's day. As we have seen before, God is presenting in this little Book of Micah a philosophy of human government, the basis of which is men of good character in positions of leadership.

"Who pluck off their skin from off them, and their flesh from off their bones." He uses a vivid illustration of their barbarous conduct against the poor.

> **Who also eat the flesh of my people, and flay their skin from off them; and they break their bones, and chop them in pieces, as for the pot, and as flesh within the caldron [Mic. 3:3].**

In other words, they are like unfeeling human cannibals in their treatment of the poor. They are unprincipled and merciless. May I say that a godless man is the last man I want to sit in judgment upon me in any matter. And, very frankly, I am thankful that I don't have to stand before you in judgment, even if you are a Christian. And you ought to be delighted that you will not have to stand before me in judgment. I believe we will fare better in the presence of the Lord Jesus Christ than we would if we were judged by mankind. My case has already been appealed to Him, and I will not have to stand before any man to be judged. It is comforting to know this.

> **Then shall they cry unto the LORD, but he will not hear them: he will even hide his face from them at that time,**

as they have behaved themselves ill in their doings [Mic. 3:4].

Who is the prophet talking about? He is talking about the leaders in Israel. As long as they had been in their high positions, they had had no regard for the human side, and they had had no real sympathy or love. Now they are in trouble because a power greater than they has come down upon them.

"Then shall they cry unto the LORD, but he will not hear them." These leaders are going to cry out to God. Isn't that interesting? We all cry out to God in times of real trouble. I have been rather amused at times—I shouldn't be, but I can't help it—when I hear of the trouble that is coming upon us today and somebody says, "May God help us!" That is interesting because they bowed Him out of His universe many years ago. God isn't mentioned much today, except in profanity, but every now and then I find people saying, "May God help us." Well, my friend, I don't know whether He will hear you or not, because in Micah's day He said to the people who had ignored Him and lived godless lives that He would not hear their cry for help. In fact, He said that He would hide His face from them. My friend, we are living in a period of the silence of God. It does not look as if God is doing much to alleviate the present world situation. Yet His grace is still abundant, and He is rich in mercy to those who will bow before Him and accept His Son as Savior.

SINS OF THE PROPHETS

Thus saith the LORD concerning the prophets that make my people err, that bite with their teeth, and cry, Peace; and he that putteth not into their mouths, they even prepare war against him [Mic. 3:5].

The false prophets were like vicious animals or like serpents with forked tongues and fangs that would poison—actually, they were worse than that because they used smooth words to comfort the people, assuring them that peace was coming.

The futile effort of man to achieve peace ought to alert us to the fact that man by his own resources cannot bring peace to the world. Just wanting it and saying often enough that it is coming and voting for it will not bring peace. Again Micah makes it very clear that it is not a surface problem. It is not that folk don't *want* peace. The problem is that the human heart is wicked, and Isaiah, a contemporary of Micah, wrote, "There is no peace, saith my God, to the wicked" (Isa. 57:21). In fact, Isaiah repeats this fact three times in the last part of his prophecy. The great climax to which he came in each of those three times was that the real problem was the *wickedness* of the human heart.

When I make the statement that we cannot have peace in our day, I generally get two or three letters from well-meaning folk. They write lovely letters that chide me for being pessimistic. They insist that we should continue to try to bring peace in the world. They are sincere and their argument sounds good, but it is one of the most false teachings abroad that *man* can make peace in *his* way. I want peace as much as anyone, but I want to go at it God's way. First of all, the individual must know what the peace of God is. How are they going to know it? "Therefore being justified by faith, we have peace with God through our Lord Jesus Christ" (Rom. 5:1). It is not possible to have peace with your fellow man until you have peace with God. The human heart cannot be trusted; it is desperately wicked (see Jer. 17:9). You and I do not know how bad we really are. We can sink lower than any other creature on earth. One of the proofs that mankind has not descended from animals is that man can sink lower than animals—animals don't go out and get drunk or beat their mates or abuse their offspring. The human race must have the peace of God in their hearts before they can bring peace to their world.

In Micah's day the false prophets were prophesying peace, while in the north Assyria was getting ready to come down upon them. In our day efforts are being made in certain sections of the world to get people to sit down at a peace table and settle their differences without going to war. Yet for about six thousand years of recorded history, mankind has gone to war and still fights—one nation against another nation, one tribe against another tribe, one family against another family, and one individual against another individual. Why do we do this? We know that it is not to the advantage of either side. But we do it because we are alienated from God and in rebellion against Him. We won't face up to the real problem, but we listen to the smooth words of false prophets who predict peace. Because they do this sort of thing, God pronounces upon them the calamities which are coming—

> **Therefore night shall be unto you, that ye shall not have a vision; and it shall be dark unto you, that ye shall not divine; and the sun shall go down over the prophets, and the day shall be dark over them [Mic. 3:6].**

"Therefore night shall be unto you." As we see in the other books of the prophets, darkness always speaks of judgment. It speaks of judgment in two different ways: the direct intervention of God in the punishment of the offender and also in the silence of God in not giving any new revelation to man.

"Ye shall not have a vision"—that is, God will not reveal any new truth to you.

"It shall be dark unto you." The judgment which is coming to them is called darkness; there will not be any light from the Word of God. There will be a cessation of prophesying.

In the New Testament the apostle Paul made reference to this in 1 Corinthians 13:8: "Charity never faileth: but whether there be prophecies, they shall fail. . . ." The English word *fail* is the Greek ekpiptō, meaning "to fall off or away." Prophecies will fail in two different ways: (1) they will not be fulfilled; and (2) God will no longer reveal anything new. There was a hiatus of approximately four hundred years between the Old Testament and the New Testament in which God was silent. The sun had gone down. Malachi, the last prophet, prophesied that the sun would come up again—"But unto you that fear my name shall the Sun of righteousness arise with healing in his wings . . ." (Mal. 4:2). Malachi would not have prophesied of the sun arising if the night had not been coming, and it did come. The people of Israel entered the long night of four hundred years until the coming of Christ. This is the same picture that Micah presents.

At the present time the United States has moved into the same position as that into which Israel had moved in Micah's day. It is easy for the very sophisticated historians to characterize as narrow-minded and bigoted the men and women who first came to settle in this country. Well, they were imperfect human beings, but even those who were not Christians had a knowledge of and a reverence for the Word of God. Both Harvard and Yale universities were founded to train ministers so that the people in this country would not be in that darkness of ignorance concerning the Word of God. Well, I tell you, their light has gone out, hasn't it? The very places that were supposed to be great educational centers and great lights for this country turned away from God a long time ago. The night is upon us today. At the universities we have had some of the worst riots this nation has ever seen. They have been the very hotbeds of darkness. It is at the university where the worship of Satan originated, and that is where it is being propagated. I have a newspaper clipping telling about a professor who is now involved in the worship of Satan and who indulges in the occult. We are in a period of time, it seems to me, when the sun of revelation has gone down. When I speak of revelation, I am talking about the illumination of the Word of God. The very centers which should be giving light from the Word of God are not doing it anymore. In fact, they are rejecting and turning their backs on God and turning to the occult. This is what Micah is talking about when he says, "Therefore night shall be unto you, that ye shall not have a vision; and it shall be dark unto you, that ye shall not divine; and the sun shall go down over the prophets, and the day shall be dark over them."

Then shall the seers be ashamed, and the diviners confounded: yea, they shall all cover their lips; for there is no answer of God [Mic. 3:7].

Micah is saying that there shall be such gross darkness that those who are false prophets will make fools of themselves because of the fact that their prophecies will not come to pass. You will recall that this was the thing Ahab discovered, only he discovered it too late. All of the false prophets told him to go and fight in the war. Only one prophet, God's man, told him that if he went to war he would not come back but would be slain. That true prophet was Micaiah. It was too bad Ahab didn't listen to him, because Ahab went to war and was slain, just as Micaiah said (see 1 Kings 22:1–28).

God's men tell it like it is, and they tell the truth. My friend, there is no use trying to cover up the sins in the church. It has become revolting to hear of the many men who are classed as religious leaders, yet are involved in reprehensible conduct, and who, under the guise of being Christians, are prospering.

We need to read again Hebrews 12:6: "For whom the Lord loveth he chasteneth, and scourgeth every son whom he receiveth." Why does the Lord do that? He does it because He doesn't want us to be illegitimate. He says to us, "I chasten you and I discipline you so that you can know and the world can know that you are My child." Did you know that William the Conqueror actually signed his name William the Bastard because he was illegitimate? I am of the opinion that many church members could sign their names the same way. You might be able to say, "I am a deacon in the church, I am a Sunday school teacher, I am a leader in the church, or I am a preacher," but you would have to write under your name what William the Conqueror wrote under his name when he signed it. You would have to admit, "I am really not a legitimate child of God. I have not really been born again. I do not really know Jesus Christ as my personal Savior. I do not love Him. I do not seek to serve Him. I am not interested in His Word at all."

In Micah's day the false prophet was in that same position. He was speaking smooth words to comfort the people. The people had itching ears, and the prophet would scratch them, you see, by saying what they wanted to hear. Then they in turn would scratch the ears of the prophet by telling him how wonderful he was. "My, what a great preacher you are because you say such nice things. Everything must be all right." They were living in luxury, but the level of immorality was frightening.

Now notice that Micah is very careful to separate himself from that group.

> But truly I am full of power by the spirit of the LORD, and
> of judgment, and of might, to declare unto Jacob his
> transgression, and to Israel his sin [Mic. 3:8].

It took intestinal fortitude to be an unpopular preacher delivering a
message the people hated, but Micah could say, "I know that the Spirit
of God is leading me to say what I am saying." It is wonderful to be in
that position, my friend.

SINS OF THE LEADERS OF JERUSALEM

In this final division, Micah turns specifically to Jerusalem. Hereto-
fore he has been speaking to the northern kingdom of Israel; but now
he bundles together the prophets, the princes, and the priests of the
southern kingdom, and he pronounces judgment upon all of them.

> Hear this, I pray you, ye heads of the house of Jacob, and
> princes of the house of Israel, that abhor judgment, and
> pervert all equity [Mic. 3:9].

He says, "Listen to me, I have something to say to you." Then he details their sins.

> They build up Zion with blood, and Jerusalem with in-
> iquity.

> The heads thereof judge for reward, and the priests
> thereof teach for hire, and the prophets thereof divine
> for money: yet will they lean upon the LORD, and say, Is
> not the LORD among us? none evil can come upon us
> [Mic. 3:10–11].

"The heads thereof judge for reward . . . the priests thereof teach for
hire . . . the prophets thereof divine for money." What is the thing that
they all have in common? Greed, covetousness. My friend, that was
the worst kind of idolatry even in the day of idols! Today we don't

have an idol sitting around—at least I hope you don't. While it is true that superstition is gaining ground and multitudes of folk are following the horoscope, we still have not reverted to the base idolatry that existed in Micah's day; yet our covetousness is idolatry. Micah brings into focus Israel's real sin: idolatry, since covetousness is idolatry. The judges were judging for reward; the priests were teaching for hire; and the prophets were divining for money. They were all doing it for what they could get out of it for themselves. They did not take God into consideration, nor did they take the people into consideration. They were willing to walk over them. No wonder the charge was made: "You eat them up like cannibals because of your greed and love of money."

When the leadership of a nation—both civil and religious—is evil, no form of government will work. This is Micah's message to us.

Therefore shall Zion for your sake be plowed as a field, and Jerusalem shall become heaps, and the mountain of the house as the high places of the forest [Mic. 3:12].

This is a prediction that for their sins there will be a complete desolation of the city of Jerusalem. Jeremiah quotes Micah as having said this (see Jer. 26:18), which is a confirmation of the prophecy. The destruction did take place when Nebuchadnezzar destroyed Jerusalem. In the first chapters of the Book of Nehemiah, we see the significance of it. When Nehemiah went back to Jerusalem, he found it in a mess. It was nothing but debris, ashes, rubble, and ruin. It seemed like a hopeless task to rebuild the city. The Talmud, which is a Jewish writing, records the fact that at the destruction of Jerusalem by Rome in A.D. 70, an officer of the Roman army (Rufus, by name) actually plowed up the foundations of the temple with a plowshare. Many scholars reject that tradition, although the Jewish historian Jerome also noted it, as did the Jewish philosopher Maimonides. Personally, I think the tradition is accurate. Both Nebuchadnezzar and Titus the Roman were certainly capable of doing a thing like that. Whether or not that particular tradition is accurate, Jerusalem even today bears the scars of the accurate fulfillment of Micah's prophecy.

CHAPTER 4

THEME: Prophecies of the last days

The little prophecy of Micah could be compared to a Jewish day in that it goes from evening to morning. It opens in the darkness of night—the first three chapters pronounce judgment, as we have seen: "Who is a God like unto thee" (Mic. 7:18) in proclaiming future judgment for past sins? But even in the darkness of judgment there was a ray of light which broke through momentarily. Now we have come to a new section, in which Micah prophesies future glory. This we will see in chapters 4 and 5. There will also be a little judgment in this section, but in the main it is glorious light with every now and then a cloud passing across the brightness of the sun.

PROPHECIES OF THE LAST DAYS

But in the last days it shall come to pass, that the mountain of the house of the LORD shall be established in the top of the mountains, and it shall be exalted above the hills; and the people shall flow unto it [Mic. 4:1].

This is a remarkable passage of Scripture and may sound familiar to you because it is similar to the second chapter of Isaiah. Micah, you may recall, was a contemporary of Isaiah, and through the years scholars have been trying to determine if Micah copied Isaiah or if Isaiah copied Micah. Candidly, I feel that such debate is a waste of time, because nobody has the answer to it. I would rather look at it this way: Since the Holy Spirit was the author, He was able to say the same things through Isaiah and through Micah; and the reason He said it twice was because of its importance. Therefore, we should look at this section very carefully.

Notice that this fourth chapter opens with the little conjunction "but," which is a connective that contrasts it to the last verse of chapter 3: "Therefore shall Zion for your sake be plowed as a field, and Jerusalem shall become heaps, and the mountain of the house as the high places of the forest."

"But in the last days." Micah is moving now beyond the destruction of Jerusalem by Nebuchadnezzar and the destruction under Titus the Roman, and beyond all other destructions, to the last days. In the Old Testament, "the last days" is a technical term with a very definite meaning. Our Lord Jesus called it "the tribulation, the great one" (see Matt. 24:21). We designate it as the Great Tribulation period, which begins "the last days." Then after the Tribulation (which will be a brief period of approximately seven years), the Lord Jesus Christ will return to the earth. In fact, His coming will end the Tribulation period, and He Himself will establish His Kingdom upon the earth. So "the last days" embrace the Tribulation, the return of Christ to the earth, and the millennial Kingdom of Christ. Therefore, when Micah says "in the last days," he has moved out and beyond all local situations, and he is looking way down into the future. The darker it became in Israel, the brighter the future appeared. And that is true for all of us. I am told that if you go far enough down in a well, you can see the stars. And when Israel hit bottom, God let them see the stars, the light out yonder in the future.

"The mountain of the house of the LORD shall be established in the top of the mountains." The word *mountain* is used both literally and figuratively. Daniel uses it in a figurative way when he says, "Thou sawest till that a stone was cut out without hands, which smote the image upon his feet that were of iron and clay, and brake them to pieces. Then was the iron, the clay, the brass, the silver, and the gold, broken to pieces together, and became like the chaff of the summer threshingfloors; and the wind carried them away, that no place was found for them: and the stone that smote the image became a great mountain, and filled the whole earth" (Dan. 2:34–35). That stone pictures Christ who is coming. "The stone . . . became a great mountain, and filled the whole earth." The mountain Daniel is talking about is Christ's Kingdom, which is to be established here upon the earth. That is the spiritual interpretation. We have no right to spiritualize a passage unless there is scriptural authority for doing so, and we do have it for this. However, I would not want to rob it of its literal sense, because the fact is that the city of Jerusalem is located upon a hill. Not only does Scripture make that clear, but all you have to do is to take a look at it. Micah is talking about Jerusalem, as we shall see. And the millennial Kingdom will be centered there. Jerusalem will be the capital of the earth.

"And people shall flow unto it." The word *flow* indicates spontaneous movement—from the desire in their hearts. Right now—as I am writing this—the flow is in the opposite direction. However, the way world conditions are changing, it could be different by the time you read this. But the point is that this prophecy of Micah's is not being fulfilled today and will not be fulfilled until the Messiah comes.

> And many nations shall come, and say, Come, and let us go up to the mountain of the LORD, and to the house of the God of Jacob; and he will teach us of his ways, and we will walk in his paths: for the law shall go forth of Zion, and the word of the LORD from Jerusalem [Mic. 4:2].

Here is another chapter, among the many chapters in the prophetic books of the Bible, which makes it clear that the present return of the Jews to the land of Israel is not a fulfillment of prophecy. In this day in which we live the nations of the world are not going to Jerusalem to hear from the Lord! Neither is the Word of the Lord going forth from Jerusalem. I could supply you with the names of several Christian missionaries in the city of Jerusalem who themselves are Jewish, but who have been persecuted for presenting Christ and the Word of God. Believe me, the Word of God is not flowing from Jerusalem!

My friend, all the current sensationalism which declares that prophecy is being fulfilled in that land just produces an itch in what I call baby Christians. They want the bottle to be warm and sweet; and, therefore, it is nice to hear that we are seeing a fulfillment of prophecy, which means that the end is just around the corner. Some folk are even setting dates for our Lord's return. Well, nobody *knows*. Although I *think* we are drawing near to the end, I have no inside information from the Lord to confirm it, and certainly there is nothing in His Word to confirm it. I wish these sensational speakers who major in prophecy would read *all* the prophecies throughout the Bible. If they would do that, it would be quite obvious to them that prophecies like Micah gives us here are not now being fulfilled. The Word of God is *not* going out from Jerusalem today. For example, no Bible society is printing Bibles in Jerusalem and sending them out to the ends of the earth! To circulate the New Testament from that place would be utterly impossible. The Word of God is not going forth from Jerusalem as Micah said it would do. The wonderful prophecies in this chapter will be fulfilled during the millennial Kingdom when Christ Himself is reigning in Jerusalem. Then the heads of the capitals of the world— Beijing, Berlin, London, Washington—will be going to Jerusalem to be taught by Christ Himself of His ways!

> **And he shall judge among many people, and rebuke**
> **strong nations afar off; and they shall beat their swords**
> **into plowshares, and their spears into pruninghooks:**
> **nation shall not lift up a sword against nation, neither**
> **shall they learn war any more [Mic. 4:3].**

"And he shall judge among many people." This again is the Lord Jesus Christ, the Messiah, when He returns to the earth the second time to reign. Imagine the nations of the world bringing their disputes to *Him* for arbitration! The things mentioned in this verse cannot come to pass until He does come.

"They shall beat their swords into plowshares, and their spears into pruninghooks." This verse appears on the building of the United Nations. Believe me, it doesn't belong there! If those boys have beaten their swords into plowshares, it only means that they have a bigger instrument with which to beat each other over the head. And if they are turning their spears into pruninghooks, they are not using them to catch fish but to gouge other nations, especially those that are weaker than they are. This verse certainly is not being fulfilled by the United Nations! They are really knocking each other out there, and there is very little agreement. It will not be fulfilled until Christ comes.

"Nation shall not lift up a sword against nation, neither shall they learn war any more." Obviously, we have not come to this position and will not until the Prince of Peace is ruling. Because He is not ruling in our day, we are not to beat our swords into plowshares; we are to keep our powder dry. This is not the time to disarm. Certainly everyone who wants peace would like to see our armaments cut back and our tax dollars going to something else, but as long as we are living in a big, bad world—not of make-believe but of reality—we need to be armed. The Lord Jesus said, ". . . a strong man armed keepeth his palace . . ." (Luke 11:21). Does he keep it by turning the other cheek? To read about turning the other cheek, you must read the Sermon on the Mount, and remember that it is the King who is speaking and He is referring to the time when He will be reigning upon the earth. When He is reigning, we can get rid of all our protection. We can even take the locks off our doors—but until then I not only have one lock on my door, I have two locks. We are living in that kind of world. These prophecies that Micah is giving are not for the present hour; they are for the last days. Let's put them in their proper context.

> But they shall sit every man under his vine and under his fig tree; and none shall make them afraid: for the mouth of the LORD of hosts hath spoken it [Mic. 4:4].

"They shall sit every man under his vine and under his fig tree; and none shall make them afraid." Do you want to tell me that this verse is being fulfilled in Israel today? In our day they are absolutely afraid. Why? Because they are not there according to fulfilled prophecy.

"For the mouth of the LORD of hosts hath spoken it." God Himself has said this. God says that when He puts them in the land, they will live in peace and prosperity.

> For all people will walk every one in the name of his god, and we will walk in the name of the LORD our God for ever and ever [Mic. 4:5].

The American Standard Version has a much better translation of this verse: "For all the peoples walk every one in the name of his god; and we will walk in the name of Jehovah our God for ever and ever." The thought is that in the past they walked after their own gods, but in the future they are going to walk in the name of Jehovah, our God.

> **In that day, saith the LORD, will I assemble her that halteth, and I will gather her that is driven out, and her that I have afflicted [Mic. 4:6].**

"In that day" reminds us that He is still speaking of the millennial Kingdom.

"Will I assemble her that halteth." Who is this whom God describes as halting, driven out, and afflicted? It is the nation Israel. Notice that He says, "That I have afflicted." It looks as if God takes the blame for that which has happened to the nation Israel.

I had a conversation with a Jewish man in front of the King David Hotel in Jerusalem several years ago. He was one of the Jews who had come out of Nazi persecution alive, although he had spent time in a concentration camp. He said that he had become an atheist. He asked, "Where was God during the time of our trouble? Why didn't He deliver us?"

I told him, "To tell the truth, I think God was around. Maybe you would like to blame Him for the trouble you had."

He replied, "I certainly do. If there is a God, He would have responded to us."

I said, "No, because you folk had an opportunity to know Him and obey Him way ahead of the rest of us. When your nation had a knowledge of the living and true God, my ancestors were heathens. One tribe was in Germany, and the other tribe was in Scotland. They were dirty, filthy, ignorant pagans, but you had the *light*. Finally some of your people brought the light to my people, and I'm grateful for it. But God has made it very clear in your own writings, your own books, that when you have a knowledge of the true and living God, you cannot turn your back on Him without being punished. If you will read your writings, you will find that not only can you blame Him for your trouble, but He is also not through with you as a nation. He intends to regather you. By that time you will have learned (and obviously you have not learned it yet) that this is God's universe and that you cannot reject the knowledge of Himself that He has given you without suffering His judgment."

My friend, our own nation is coming to this same position and condition, and it alarms me. In this land of ours there is a growing ignorance of the Word of God. Even worse than that, the Word of God is being ridiculed and made light of. A comedian says, "The Devil made me do it." This is simply not true. You don't do evil because the Devil made you do it. You do evil because you have an old nature that is as mean and as alienated and as far from God as it can possibly be. Also I hear it flippantly said, "I'll tell God on you!" Well, of course, you don't have to tell Him about somebody else's sin. He already knows it, and He knows yours as well. My friend, we cannot make light of Him and reject Him without experiencing His judgment. In Micah's day He took the blame for afflicting Israel, and He has not asked me to apologize for Him or to try to explain away that statement. This ought to serve as a warning to us as a nation.

And I will make her that halted a remnant, and her that was cast far off a strong nation: and the LORD shall reign over them in mount Zion from henceforth, even for ever [Mic. 4:7].

"I will make her that halted a remnant." Never throughout the long history of Israel did 100 percent of the nation worship God. Always only a remnant was faithful to Him. God always preserved a remnant. Actually, it was a remnant of those which came out of Egypt that entered the land. Practically the entire generation that came out of Egypt died in the wilderness. It was their children who entered the land. God preserved a remnant. Even in Elijah's day God had a faithful remnant. Elijah was very pessimistic. He cried, "Lord, I only am left" (see 1 Kings 19:10). But God told him, "You aren't the only one; I have seven thousand in these mountains who have not bowed the knee to Baal." Because they were hiding from Ahab and Jezebel, Elijah didn't know about them. (And I am of the opinion that in our day there are more believers than we think there are. There are many believers like those seven thousand. Although we don't hear about them, they are true believers.) Also, there was a remnant of believers at the coming of Christ; although the leaders of the nation rejected Him and had Him crucified, there was a remnant that received Him. Later, on the day of Pentecost, a great company turned to Christ; yet it was a remnant. It always has been a remnant. Coming down to our day, there is a remnant even in the church that bears His name. Although I have made the statement that I think there are more believers in our world than we realize, it is also true that in the church there is only a remnant of true believers in Christ.

Many of us would be surprised if we knew how few church members were genuine believers even though they are quite active in Christian circles and in Christian service. Many people in our affluent society have become church members. We are living in a period that has produced a lot of pseudo-saints. They are not genuine by any means. They have not been born again. The Book of Hebrews makes it very clear that ". . . whom the Lord loveth he chasteneth . . ." (Heb. 12:6). And every son whom He receives, He is going to put through the fire. He is going to test him. If you have some metal which you think is gold, you can take it to the assayer's office. He will put the metal under the heat so that you will find out whether what you have is gold or something else. And God puts the heat to those who are His own. The day of persecution is going to come to church members, and it will reveal quickly who are the true believers and who are not. God has a remnant in the church today.

Also in our day there is a remnant of believers among the people of Israel—probably more than we realize. In every nation there is a remnant of true believers, although they may not be identified with a local church. Unfortunately, the actions of some church members are shutting the door to a great many believers. Yet God always has His faithful remnant. The word remnant in Scripture is very important; don't just rush over it.

In Micah's day God is saying that of the afflicted ones He will make a remnant; He will regather them and make them "a strong nation: and the LORD shall reign over them in mount Zion from henceforth, even for ever."

> And thou, O tower of the flock, the strong hold of the
> daughter of Zion, unto thee shall it come, even the first
> dominion; the kingdom shall come to the daughter of
> Jerusalem [Mic. 4:8].

"O tower of the flock, the strong hold of the daughter of Zion." God is probably addressing the land itself, informing it that its former dominion under David and Solomon will be restored, the far greater Kingdom of the Messiah shall come. This has not happened yet; the Kingdom has not come. If the people of Israel are back in their land for anything, they are back there for the Great Tribulation period. The Kingdom is still in the far future.

THE NEAR FUTURE

At this point a cloud passes over the sun. A great many Bible scholars believe the next two verses refer to the Babylonian captivity.

> Now why dost thou cry out aloud? is there no king in
> thee? is thy counsellor perished? for pangs have taken
> thee as a woman in travail.

> Be in pain, and labour to bring forth, O daughter of
> Zion, like a woman in travail: for now shalt thou go
> forth out of the city, and thou shalt dwell in the field,
> and thou shalt go even to Babylon; there shalt thou be
> delivered; there the Lord shall redeem thee from the
> hand of thine enemies [Mic. 4:9–10].

This is so specific that I feel it could refer to nothing else but the Babylonian captivity which was coming to the southern kingdom. When Micah directs his remarks to the "daughter of Zion," he refers to the southern kingdom of Judah. The word that interests me here is *travail*. Frankly, I can't speak about travail firsthand. One half of the human family does not know what it is to travail in birth. Only the women know about that. The only thing I know about birth pangs is what I saw my own wife go through and what I have been told by others. Birth pangs are frightful. They are something no person could bear for a long period of time. It has to be temporary.

The picture Micah gives us here is that of Nebuchadnezzar taking Jerusalem. He came to that city three times, and the third time he destroyed the temple area, left it in wrack and ruin, leveled the city, and burned it. The suffering of the people of Judah is described as a woman in travail, a woman with birth pangs. This had to be a brief period or the nation would not have continued to exist. That kind of trouble could not go on forever because the people could not have endured it. It would have been too frightful, too terrible. For this same reason the Great Tribulation period must be brief. The Lord Jesus Christ made that clear: "And except those days should be shortened, there should no flesh be saved: but for the elect's sake those days shall be shortened" (Matt. 24:22).

"Thou shalt go forth out of the city, and thou shalt dwell in the field, and thou shalt go even to Babylon." When Nebuchadnezzar captured the city, the remaining inhabitants fled and tried to live in the fields. Eventually they were taken captive to Babylon.

Let me call your attention to the fact that Micah in these two verses is looking beyond the Assyrian captivity of Israel to the later captivity of Judah by Babylon. However, in the next breath he predicts deliverance: "There shalt thou be delivered; there the LORD shall redeem thee from the hand of thine enemies." Although they shall be captives in Babylon, God will deliver them from there. We know from history that God did deliver them by the hand of Cyrus (see Isa. 44:28; 2 Chron. 36:22-23). The point that Micah is making here is that the travail and suffering of God's people will end in joy.

THE DISTANT FUTURE

Now in this closing section Micah moves ahead to the far distant future, the time of the Great Tribulation and specifically to the final war, the War (not the battle) of Armageddon.

Now also many nations are gathered against thee, that say, Let her be defiled, and let our eye look upon Zion [Mic. 4:11].

"Many nations are gathered against thee"—the mention of many nations makes it clear that Micah has moved away from the Babylonian invasion and is speaking of something else here. The many nations gathered against Jerusalem are mentioned by several other prophets. For example: Joel 3; Zechariah 12 and 14; Ezekiel 38 and 39 all refer to the War of Armageddon during the Great Tribulation period.

But they know not the thoughts of the LORD, neither understand they his counsel: for he shall gather them as the sheaves into the floor [Mic. 4:12].

"They know not the thoughts of the LORD, neither understand they his counsel." They do not know what God is going to do. They are coming against Israel blindly, unaware that God is bringing them there for judgment.

Arise and thresh, O daughter of Zion: for I will make thine horn iron, and I will make thy hoofs brass: and thou shalt beat in pieces many people: and I will consecrate their gain unto the LORD, and their substance unto the Lord of the whole earth [Mic. 4:13].

"Arise and thresh, O daughter of Zion." The nations of the world are as sheaves for the threshing floor, and Israel will do the threshing. Today Israel is a weak nation and absolutely dependent upon other nations, but in that day they are going to be dependent upon the Lord. Psalm 75:6 says, "For promotion cometh neither from the east, nor from the west, nor from the south." Psalm 75:7 goes on to say, "But God is the judge: he putteth down one, and setteth up another." In that day help for Israel will not come from the north (Russia), or from the south (Egypt), or from the west (Europe or the United States), or from the east (China and the Arab countries). Their help will come from the Lord who made heaven and earth.

These final three verses look forward to the war which concludes the Great Tribulation period, the War of Armageddon.

CHAPTER 5

THEME: Prophecy of the first coming of Christ

This chapter continues the subject begun in chapter 4: prophesying future glory because of past promises. In chapter 4 we saw prophecies regarding the last days; now we shall see prophecies regarding the first coming of Christ.

> **Now gather thyself in troops, O daughter of troops: he hath laid siege against us: they shall smite the judge of Israel with a rod upon the cheek [Mic. 5:1].**

In the Hebrew Scriptures this verse concludes chapter 4. Frankly, I feel that it belongs there, not here, and that it continues the thought of chapter 4 verse 9 regarding the Babylonian captivity. You will recall that Micah projects the horrors of the Babylonian invasion right on down to the "last days," that is, to the Great Tribulation period and the War of Armageddon. Now in the verse before us, he again picks up the thought of the Babylonian invasion.

"He hath laid siege against us" refers, I believe, to the siege of the Babylonian army against Jerusalem.

"They shall smite the judge of Israel with a rod upon the cheek." There are those who take the position that the "judge" refers to the Lord Jesus Christ. However, in the Gospel record we read that they smote Him with their hands, not with a rod. Neither was Christ smitten in any siege. He was not smitten by a foreign enemy but by His own people. I do not believe that this can refer to the mistreatment of Christ at His first coming.

It seems obvious to me that the "judge of Israel" refers to the last king of the Davidic kingdom, Zedekiah. In 2 Kings 25:7 we read, "And they slew the sons of Zedekiah before his eyes, and put out the eyes of Zedekiah, and bound him with fetters of brass, and carried him to Babylon." I believe that Micah is referring to the shameful treatment which Zedekiah received at that time. It denotes what looks to be the very end of the Davidic line. However, Zedekiah was not in the direct line. You will recall that Jehoiakim rebelled against the king of Babylon. He stood against him at first; then Nebuchadnezzar, king of Babylon, took Jehoiakim into captivity. Then Jehoiachin was put on the throne. Later, he too was taken captive. In 2 Kings 24:15 we read, "And he carried away Jehoiachin to Babylon, and the king's mother, and the king's wives, and his officers, and the mighty of the land, those carried he into captivity from Jerusalem to Babylon." This was the Davidic line which was carried into captivity, and out of this line came both Joseph and Mary, the mother of the Lord Jesus. Then Nebuchadnezzar put Zedekiah (the uncle of Jehoiachin) on the throne at Jerusalem. When *he* rebelled against Babylon, Nebuchadnezzar became tired of fooling with the line of kings at Jerusalem; so he took Zedekiah, slew all of his sons before his eyes, and carried him into captivity.

You might assume from this devastating experience that the Davidic line had come to an end and that the promise God made to David, that one was to come in his line who would reign forever, could never be fulfilled.

This brings us to a remarkable verse that is in contrast to all we have been considering.

PROPHECY OF THE FIRST COMING OF CHRIST

Now this verse is part of the Christmas story; and, if you are not reading this during December, you may feel that you have chosen an inappropriate time. However, we can be almost sure that Jesus was not born on December 25. That day was chosen to try to identify His birth with the winter solstice. But it is more likely that He was born in the spring, because in December the shepherds would not be out on the hillsides with their sheep. The sheep would be sheltered in the caves which are located all along that area. Around A.D. 532 a calendar was set up, which is a reasonable facsimile of the one we use today. It was set up incorrectly for the number of days in the year, and that is why we have a leap year every now and then. In 1752 the calendar was jumped ahead eleven days. George Washington was not born on February 22; he was actually born on February 11. Therefore, a person could not be sure that Jesus Christ was born on December 25 even if all of the other circumstances fit into it. This raises a question about observing the Sabbath Day, too. Which day is the Sabbath Day? Actually, it is not important, nor is the exact day of Jesus' birth important. The time of the year is immaterial. It is the *place* that is all important. Christ was born in Bethlehem. That is the historical fact. This fact has been authenticated by history.

> **But thou, Beth-lehem Ephratah, though thou be little among the thousands of Judah, yet out of thee shall he come forth unto me that is to be ruler in Israel; whose goings forth have been from of old, from everlasting [Mic. 5:2].**

"But" is a little conjunction that presents the other side of the coin. "But thou, Beth-lehem." In spite of what happened to Zedekiah and the Davidic line—which went into captivity and finally returned to the land of Israel as peasants—the one in David's line *is* coming.

"But thou, Beth-lehem Ephratah"—since there were two Bethlehems, the word *ephratah*, meaning "fruitful", is added to distinguish between them. Micah named the place where Christ was to be born seven hundred years *before* He was born there. After seven hundred years, with so many intervening events, there was little likelihood that one in the line of David could be born in Bethlehem. It was almost entirely out of the question. The odds were against it. No members of the family of David were living in Bethlehem any longer. They were scattered. The Dispersion had driven them from the land. There was one family in the line of David living in Nazareth; yet Bethlehem must be the place where the Son of God was to be born, according to Micah. This prophecy was the sole basis on which the scribes directed the wise men to Bethlehem. The scribes quoted from the prophecy of Micah because they believed that it was the place where He would be born, although they didn't believe it would be fulfilled at that time.

The circumstances which led up to the birth of Jesus in Bethlehem are so familiar to us that we may not realize how remarkable they were. The record in Luke's Gospel gives us some of the details: Caesar Augustus signed the tax bill which moved Mary out of Nazareth. If that little donkey on which Mary rode had stumbled and Mary had fallen, Jesus would probably have been born somewhere along the route. But—I say this very carefully—that little donkey could not have stumbled, because seven hundred years earlier Micah had written that Jesus would be born in Bethlehem. The little donkey got her there on schedule; it was timed from eternity. It was more punctual and precise than any jet plane could be in our day.

"Out of thee shall he come forth unto me." The words *unto me* indicate that this One was coming to do the will of the Father and to accomplish His plan.

"Whose goings forth have been from of old, from everlasting." His birth, the Incarnation, has to do with His humanity. He clothed Himself in humanity when He came to Bethlehem. But His existence was before His birth.

Isaiah, a contemporary of Micah, verifies this: ". . . Behold, a virgin shall conceive, and bear a son, and shall call his name Immanuel" (Isa. 7:14). And he has more to say of this coming one: "For unto us a child is born, unto us a son is given . . ." (Isa. 9:6). When Isaiah wrote "unto us," he was not thinking of the United States; it was Israel that he had in mind. "A child is born"— that's His humanity. "A son is given"—not born, because this speaks of His divinity. The "child" was born in Bethlehem, but the "Son" was "from everlasting."

The psalmist mentions this: "Before the mountains were brought forth, or ever thou hadst formed the earth and the world, even from everlasting to everlasting, thou art God" (Ps. 90:2). The Hebrew language expresses this very vividly: "from the vanishing point in the past to the vanishing point in the future, thou art God." Just as far back as you can go in your thinking, He is God. He came out of eternity. He is the eternal Son of God.

In Proverbs 8:23 we find, "I was set up from everlasting, from the beginning, or ever the earth was." "Set up" in this verse means "anointed" and could read, "I was anointed from everlasting, from the beginning, or ever the earth was." The next two verses say, "When there were no depths, I was brought forth; when there were no fountains abounding with water. Before the mountains were settled, before the hills was I brought forth" (Prov. 8:24–25). Before there was any creation, He was God; yet into creation He came, at the appointed time, into a little out-of-the-way town, Bethlehem.

The Lord Jesus said, "I came forth from the Father, and am come into the world: again, I leave the world, and go to the Father" (John 16:28). His goings forth have been of old. He is the everlasting God. He told the Pharisees, ". . . Before Abraham was, I am" (John 8:58). Christ appeared many times in the Old Testament. Go back to the creation. In John 1:3 we read concerning Christ, "All things were made by him; and without him was not any thing made that was made." He was the Creator. In Colossians 1:16 we read this about our Lord, "For by him were all things created, that are in heaven, and that are in earth, visible and invisible, whether they be thrones, or dominions, or principalities, or powers: all things were created by him, and for him." In the Garden of Eden He was the voice of the Lord God walking in the garden in the cool of the day. He was the articulation of God. He was the Word of God. He was the communication from God to man. We find Him in pursuit of man throughout the Old Testament. He appeared to Moses in the burning bush. He said, "I have come down to deliver you." He was the Redeemer. You see, what Micah is saying here is of tremendous significance. Although He was born in Bethlehem almost two thousand years ago, His goings forth have been from old, from everlasting.

We have been considering His preincarnation; now let's look again at His incarnation, His humanity. When God came to Bethlehem, He got something He never had before, and that was the name of Jesus. He received a humanity, and Jesus was His human name. He was Jehovah. That is the name of deity. He is Jesus now, and He is a Savior. He came out of Bethlehem to save. Remember, the angels said to the shepherds, "For unto you is born this day in the city of David a Saviour, which is Christ the Lord" (Luke 2:11). Matthew 1:23 says, "Behold, a virgin shall be with child, and shall bring forth a son, and they shall call his name Emmanuel, which being interpreted is, God with us." But His name was to be Jesus. He can't be Jesus unless He is Emmanuel, which means "God with us." He must be a man to take our place, to be our representative, to die a substitutionary death.

In the books of the prophets are many predictions about the coming of the Messiah which are totally unrelated and seem even to contradict each other. How could they all come to pass? Although *Bethlehem* was designated as Christ's birthplace, connected with His birth we are told that there will be weeping in *Ramah*, a place north of Bethlehem. Also, He is to be called out of *Egypt*, and He is to be called a *Nazarene*. It seems utterly impossible for all of these prophecies to be true. How can they all fit into place? Well, Matthew gives the account and, without any strain on the circumstances, all of these things come together normally and naturally—let me change that to supernaturally. God was overruling.

As you can see, Micah 5:2 is a very remarkable verse, and we have only stayed on the surface of it.

Now we come to an interval which takes place between the time of Christ's rejection and the time of His return as the King to rule on this earth.

Therefore will he give them up, until the time that she which travaileth hath brought forth: then the remnant of his brethren shall return unto the children of Israel [Mic. 5:3].

You may think that this verse still has reference to the birth of Christ. Well, it is true that it speaks of the fact that Mary travailed, but you can't read this passage without realizing that it also refers to the nation of Israel. It speaks not only of their worldwide dispersion—they were scattered by the judgment of God—but of their travail. The Great Tribulation period is the travail through which the nation must pass. "Then the remnant of his brethren shall return unto the children of Israel." The Jews will be regathered from their worldwide dispersion.

And he shall stand and feed in the strength of the Lord, in the majesty of the name of the Lord his God; and they

shall abide: for now shall he be great unto the ends of the earth [Mic. 5:4].

Here the Lord Jesus is depicted as the Shepherd who feeds His flock. He is the Shepherd to the church, and He is also the Shepherd to the nation Israel. The One who was born in Bethlehem, the One who was rejected, will feed His flock. I can't think of anything that sets Him forth more wonderfully than the figure of the shepherd. It speaks of His care, His protection, and His salvation. He is the *Good* Shepherd who will lay down His life for the sheep (see Ps. 22); He is the *Great* Shepherd who keeps His sheep even today (see Ps. 23); and He is the *Chief* Shepherd who is coming in glory (see Ps. 24). His entire ministry is set forth under the office of a shepherd.

And this man shall be the peace, when the Assyrian shall come into our land: and when he shall tread in our palaces, then shall we raise against him seven shepherds, and eight principal men [Mic. 5:5].

"The Assyrian," as we find in the prophecy of Isaiah, sets forth the enemies that shall come up against the nation Israel in the last days. In Micah's day the Assyrian was brutal, and he did take the northern kingdom into captivity.

"Then shall we raise against him seven shepherds, and eight principal men." The two numbers seem to denote the fact of fullness and that God will make adequate provision for them. These two numbers carry that meaning in other instances (see Prov. 6:16; Eccl. 11:2).

And they shall waste the land of Assyria with the sword, and the land of Nimrod in the entrances thereof: thus shall he deliver us from the Assyrian, when he cometh into our land, and when he treadeth within our borders [Mic. 5:6].

"They shall waste the land of Assyria with the sword" continues the prediction of the last days when "the Assyrian" represents the confederacy of nations which will come against Israel at the end of the Tribulation period. Israel, strengthened by their Shepherd, will not only repulse the attack but will carry the battle into enemy territory.

It is interesting to see how Micah completely sets forth Christ: first, as the One to be born in Bethlehem. When He was born on earth, He came in humility. We need to note that He humbled Himself (see Phil. 2:5–8). We don't humble ourselves; sometimes some other people humble us, but Christ humbled Himself. There was an emptying on the part of Christ. Of what did He empty Himself? Not His deity. That little baby, reclining so helplessly on His mother's bosom, could have spoken this universe out of existence. He is God of very God and man of very man, but He limited Himself. Self-limitation was something that He took willingly. We do not limit ourselves willingly. In fact, we expand ourselves. We are aggressive. We want to win. We want to be on top. Man is self-assertive. He is self-centered. He is self-ish. But Jesus Christ is the Shepherd. He was born not in a royal city or in the capital, but in the insignificant town of Bethlehem—and in a *stable*. That is no place for a king to be born! When Christ came to earth, He emptied Himself of His glory. Second, Micah indicates that He is the eternal one "whose goings forth have been from . . . everlasting." Third, Micah depicts Him as the Shepherd who came to die for His sheep and to watch over His own. And finally, when He comes again, He will be the Chief Shepherd, coming in might and power and glory to deliver His people.

> **And the remnant of Jacob shall be in the midst of many people as a dew from the Lord, as the showers upon the grass, that tarrieth not for man, nor waiteth for the sons of men [Mic. 5:7].**

The dew and rain refer to the blessing the people of Israel will be among the nations.

> **And the remnant of Jacob shall be among the Gentiles in the midst of many people as a lion among the beasts of the forest, as a young lion among the flocks of sheep:**

> who, if he go through, both treadeth down, and teareth
> in pieces, and none can deliver [Mic. 5:8].

This certainly does not depict the people of Israel in our day. Israel has been in a precarious position for years. But God promises that in the future, when Israel is obeying the Lord and is in fellowship with Him, He will make them the head and not the tail of the nations (see Deut. 28:13).

> Thine hand shall be lifted up upon thine adversaries,
> and all thine enemies shall be cut off [Mic. 5:9].

In that day God is going to give them victory over their enemies.

> And it shall come to pass in that day, saith the LORD, that
> I will cut off thy horses out of the midst of thee, and I
> will destroy thy chariots [Mic. 5:10].

Now, just in case an amillennialist is applying this to some other time, Micah wants to make sure you realize that this will come to pass "in that day," which is still future.

> And I will cut off the cities of thy land, and throw down
> all thy strong holds [Mic. 5:11].

This is thought to mean that God will remove all the things on which Israel had leaned for support—horses and chariots and fortified cities. They won't need them anymore, for their Messiah is bringing peace to earth.

> And I will cut off witchcrafts out of thine hand; and
> thou shalt have no more soothsayers:
>
> Thy graven images also will I cut off, and thy standing
> images out of the midst of thee; and thou shalt no more
> worship the work of thine hands [Mic. 5:12-13].

He is going to get rid of idolatry and false religion. They will worship
only the living and true God.

> **And I will pluck up thy groves out of the midst of thee:**
> **so will I destroy thy cities [Mic. 5:14].**

As we have seen, the "groves" were places of idol worship.

> **And I will execute vengeance in anger and fury upon**
> **the heathen, such as they have not heard [Mic. 5:15].**

"The heathen" are the nations who are persecuting His people. The
Messiah will bring blessing and peace to the remnant of Israel and to
the remnant of the other nations of the world who turn to Him, but He
will "execute vengeance in anger and fury upon the heathen"—this, I
believe, refers to the Great Tribulation period.

CHAPTER 6

THEME: Pleading present repentance because of past redemption

Chapter 6 begins Micah's third and final message to the nations of the world and to Israel in particular. Although chapters 6 and 7 are one message, I have taken the privilege of dividing these last two chapters and of making a major division out of each one of them.

PLEADING PRESENT REPENTANCE BECAUSE OF PAST REDEMPTION

Hear ye now what the Lord saith; Arise, contend thou before the mountains, and let the hills hear thy voice [Mic. 6:1].

This section begins as the other major sections of this book have begun: "Hear ye now what the Lord saith." This is a call not only to the northern kingdom, but again I take it that it is also a call to the entire world to "hear." God will now register His complaint against Israel. God has a contention with His people Israel, and from it we can learn great lessons.

"Arise, contend thou before the mountains, and let the hills hear thy voice." This is an expression that we find several times in the writings of the prophets. This is actually a call to nature, a call, it says, to the mountains and to the hills. But I believe that there is also an application here that we see elsewhere in Scripture, too. A mountain represents a great kingdom, and a hill represents a lesser kingdom. I would say, therefore, that this is a call not only to nature but also to the *nations* of the world. In other words, here is a message which is applicable to all the nations of the world.

Hear ye, O mountains, the Lord's controversy, and ye strong foundations of the earth: for the Lord hath a con-

troversy with his people, and he will plead with Israel [Mic. 6:2].

"Hear ye, O mountains, the LORD's controversy"—the nations of the world are to hear. "And ye strong foundations of the earth"—that is, the great peoples and nations of the world which have been in existence for thousands of years and yet have been far from God. God now gives a message to them.

"For the LORD hath a controversy with his people, and he will plead with Israel." God has a controversy with His people, and He is actually calling them into court.

Then God does a very startling and surprising thing. When He goes into court, instead of immediately lodging a charge against them, He says, "What am I guilty of?" Can you imagine this condescension of Almighty God to little man down here on this earth!

O my people, what have I done unto thee? and wherein have I wearied thee? testify against me [Mic. 6:3].

In other words, God is saying to them, "Why have you turned from Me? Why have you rejected Me? What have I done to you?" We find this question again in the prophecy of Malachi, the last book of the Old Testament. After their captivity, the people returned to the land and became very blasé, very sophisticated. They forgot about the Babylonian captivity. The city of Jerusalem had been rebuilt, and they were enjoying prosperity again. When Malachi spoke to them, they said, "Well, to tell the truth, this going through the religious rituals is very boring indeed, and it's wearisome." I would more or less agree with them in that, but the problem was not with God—the problem was with them. Micah is going to be very specific here as to the real problem.

God had asked the people to testify against Him and to tell Him what He has done. Now He is going to tell them what He has done to them. What is it that God has done? Has He been ugly to them? Has He mistreated them? Did He take them down to the land of Egypt and leave them there and forget about them? He could have done that. He didn't have to deliver them out of the land of Egypt, but He did deliver them. Listen to Him—

For I brought thee up out of the land of Egypt, and redeemed thee out of the house of servants; and I sent before thee Moses, Aaron, and Miriam [Mic. 6:4].

"For I brought thee up out of the land of Egypt, and redeemed thee out of the house of servants." They had been slaves, and God says, "I redeemed you. I didn't do you wrong. I didn't harm you, but I redeemed you. You were slaves, bending under the yoke of the taskmaster down in the land of Egypt, and there was no one to deliver you. You were not an attractive people; you were a slave people. You had dropped down to the lowest level of humanity, but I loved you and redeemed you out of the house of servants."

"And I sent before thee Moses, Aaron, and Miriam." God says, "I gave you leadership to lead you out of the land—Moses, Aaron, and Miriam." It is interesting that Miriam is mentioned here. I would like to call to the attention of the women's liberation movement the fact that God did not pass them by. Miriam was one of the leaders out of the land of Egypt. She was on a par with Aaron, but she was not on a par with Moses because Moses was the one that God had chosen. Actually, at one time, Miriam wanted to lead a rebellion against her own brother. When the people got out into the wilderness, Moses really took charge, for he was leading under God. But Miriam said, "Who is he to tell me anything? I remember when he was a little, bitty fellow and Mother and I took him down to the river and put him in the bullrushes because he would have been put to death by Pharaoh. I stayed at a distance, and I watched over him. Who does he think he is to tell me what to do?" I guess Miriam was the first women's liberationist that we ever had. But she *was* a leader, and she was chosen of God. I have a notion that she had a real ministry with the women of Israel. Can you imagine the problems that would arise with the women and children on that wilderness march? There would be problems that Moses would not know too much about. So Miriam must have been a great help.

The people of Israel in Micah's day complained that they were weary, tired of worshiping God. They said, "After all, what has He done for us?" So God went back and recited their history. God is pleading from His heart with these people—

O my people, remember now what Balak king of Moab consulted, and what Balaam the son of Beor answered him from Shittim unto Gilgal; that ye may know the righteousness of the LORD [Mic. 6:5].

What we have here is the reminder of a very wonderful incident that goes back to the time when the children of Israel were ready to pass into the Promised Land. They had had to go all the way around Edom because Edom would not let them through their land. God led them around Edom, and then they came to Moab. The king of Moab at that time was Balak. Balak wanted to curse the children of Israel, and he hired the prophet Balaam who was a lover of money. Balaam was a hired preacher; yet he was a prophet who seemed to have information from God. God certainly spoke through him, but God finally judged him.

Balaam was called in by Balak to curse the children of Israel. "Balaam the son of Beor answered him from Shittim unto Gilgal." Shittim was the last camping spot before they entered Moab after Balaam began his ministry against them. Gilgal was the first place they camped when they got into the Promised Land. I will not go back over each of the prophecies which Balaam gave but will only say that each time he could not curse Israel—God would not let him curse Israel.

Balak took Balaam up to a mountain, and as he looked down at the camp of Israel, Balaam said, "How shall I curse what God hath not cursed? . . ." (Num. 23:8). God was not doing them evil; God was on their side. Now, if you had gone down into the camp, you would have found they were not perfect—God was dealing with them and with their sin down there—but no enemy on the outside was going to find fault with them. The children of Israel did not know that there was an enemy trying to curse them and that God was protecting and defending them. Even old Balaam had to say, "How shall I curse, whom God hath not cursed? I am not able to do it." God did not permit them to be cursed (see Num. 22—24).

The wonderful thing for the child of God today is that we are told that we have an Advocate with the Father, Jesus Christ, the Righteous One (see 1 John 2:1). God deals with His children personally. I know that He has dealt with me and has done so severely. I am confident that the cancer which I had was a judgment of God upon me. I accept it as that from Him, and I thank Him for hearing prayers for my healing. But I am also very thankful that I have an Advocate, Jesus Christ the Righteous, who defends me. He is on my side; He is my Advocate. He is the one who says that I am His child, that I am in the family of God. He is not going to let anyone on the outside curse me.

May I say to you, this ought to answer the superstitious and wild views that are circulating today that God's children can be demon-possessed. However, I do believe that the Devil can oppress the child of God and give him a whole lot of trouble. He can certainly deceive you and make life miserable for you, but no demon is going to possess you if you are truly God's child—because you have an Advocate. It does not matter who you are; if you are a child of God, He's on your side, and He is defending you. When it seemed like the whole world had turned against him at one time, Martin Luther said, "One with God is a majority." I am on the side of the majority. How about you? That is the important question.

God is telling His people here, "I have defended you. I defended you even when Balaam attempted to curse you." Balak got disgusted with Balaam as he took him to the top of four mountains one by one, and Balaam could not curse Israel. But he did give some awful advice to Balak. He said, "Since you can't curse them, and you can't fight them, join them." It's the same old story, "If you can't fight 'em, join 'em." Balaam told the king of Moab, "Go down and intermarry with them." And that is exactly what happened—and that introduced the idolatry of Moab among the people of Israel. All of this happened because of the advice of a false prophet.

I want to say something very carefully at this point. Today we are getting a whole lot of so-called marriage counseling from false "prophets." I hear a great deal of it second-hand. My friend, much of it doesn't happen to be scriptural. I know that it is based on pulling out a little verse here and a little verse there, and you can build quite a case that way. But may I say that the only thing which is going to make a marriage work is *love*. If you can look at her and say, "I love you," and she can look back at you and say, "I love you," then, my friend, the Word of God will give you all you need to solve your problems.

God reminds Israel that He is a righteous God, but He was *defending* them. He was on *their* side. And it is wonderful to have God on our side today.

In each chapter of this book we have found a wonderful, unusual passage, and we are coming now to another in verses 6–8 of this chapter. The liberals delight especially in verse 8, saying, "This is what pure religion is. This is the greatest statement in the Old Testament." I rather agree with the liberals that it is a great statement, but I do not agree with them in the interpretation of it.

God has pleaded with these people to come back to Him, to repent of their gross negligence and sins, and to turn to Him. He has cited His redemption of them in the past, how He redeemed them out of the land of Egypt and brought them through the wilderness. Now the people have four questions that they ask, and they are good questions. The answer to them is all-important.

This is a very important passage of Scripture, because it has been used and abused by the liberals today probably more than any other passage. This is a wonderful section, but we need to be very careful to keep it in the context of what Micah is talking about here, especially as it relates to the Old Testament as a whole.

I am confident that every person who believes in a god wants to ask the question, "How am I going to approach him?" Unless you are an atheist, that has to be a question which would cross your mind. The pagan nations of the past and the heathen of the present have asked that question, and they have answered it. The pagan viewpoint is first of all revealed in their idols—they're horrible-looking. Their viewpoint is also revealed in the fact that when trouble comes they think he's angry, and they've got to do something to appease him. Today that is even the viewpoint of the pagan and heathen in my own sophisticated, civilized country. The children of Israel here ask a question, and it is a legitimate question, one that the average man would ask.

Wherewith shall I come before the LORD, and bow myself before the high God? shall I come before him with burnt offerings, with calves of a year old? [Mic. 6:6].

The people's first question is: "Wherewith shall I come before the LORD, and bow myself before the high God?" In other words, "What is wrong with God? Why is He displeased with us? We're going through the rituals and the liturgy and the rites of religion. We are going through an outward form, and it is the form which He gave us to go through." But God had also given them a relationship with Himself which they had lost.

Again, the question is: "Wherewith shall I come before the LORD, and bow myself before the high God? What can I bring to God? What can I give Him? He's way up yonder—I'm way down here. How am I going to reach Him? How am I going to communicate with Him? How am I going to make contact with Him? How will I please Him? And—how will I be saved?" The Philippian jailer, who was as pagan as they come, asked, "What must I do to be saved? How can I be right with God?" This is a good question. There is nothing wrong with the question.

The people's second question is: "Shall I come before him with burnt offerings, with calves of a year old?" God had required sacrifices of them. God had given them, in the first part of the Book of Leviticus, five offerings which they were to make, which were to be their approach to Him. So they asked the question, "Will it be adequate simply to go through the form of religion?" Man's reasoning always degenerates down to one thing: "I have to *do* something for God. He wants me to do something." May I say, this probably reveals the proud heart of man more than anything else. We want to do something for God. We feel very warm on the inside when we are generous and make a gift. The unsaved man says, "I go to church; in fact, I'm a church member. I give generously to the church. When they ask me to do something, I do it. I'm a civilized man; I don't go around hitting people on the head. I'm considered a pretty good Joe. I'm a fellow that everybody likes. Now what in the world does God want of me? Shall I do something else? I feel like I should do something."

You see, we have the whole thing backwards. We ask, "What must I *do* to be saved?" The people came to the Lord Jesus and asked, ". . . What shall we do, that we might work the works of God?" And the Lord Jesus said, ". . . This is the work of God, that ye believe on him whom he hath sent" (John 6:28–29). He is saying, ". . . Believe on the Lord Jesus Christ, and thou shalt be saved . . ." (Acts 16:31). That is the only work that God is asking you to do—*believe*. Faith is just about the opposite of works. Saving faith produces works, but it certainly does not originate salvation. Your works have nothing to do with your salvation. This is the second question of the children of Israel, and it is the normal question of man.

The people now ask a third question—

Will the Lord be pleased with thousands of rams, or with ten thousands of rivers of oil? shall I give my firstborn for my transgression, the fruit of my body for the sin of my soul? [Mic. 6:7].

"Will the Lord be pleased with thousands of rams, or with ten thousands of rivers of oil?" Now that is really being generous! In other words, they ask, "Is it because we haven't done enough for God? Should we do more for God to try to please Him?" We hear the same question asked today. Years ago I used to play volleyball with a wealthy man who was a member of the YMCA with me in Nashville, Tennessee. It was near Christmastime, and he told me, "I want you to know what my religion is. I believe in being generous. Every Christmas I give my employees a bonus, and I give to this cause and that cause and the other cause. I give to my church, too. Now what else could God ask of me?" In other words, "I go the second mile. I'm a big spender as far as the Lord is concerned. I'm doing all this—what else could He ask me to do?" This is the question: Is it that we need to be very generous in what we do? Is that our problem? Many folk express it this way: "Well, maybe I'm not doing enough. I just don't feel like

I'm right with God. I don't seem to be doing enough." These are sincere people; but because they are not saved, although they are church members, they feel that they need to do a little bit more than they are doing.

This line of thinking is something that the liberal preacher can work on; he can use a psychological approach. He can say, "Now look here, you folk are not doing enough." And so the fellow digs down a little deeper in his pocket, especially if he is a man of means, and says, "I'll give a little bit more. God will be tickled to death with that. My, He is sure going to be pleased with me." Just like Little Jack Horner, man becomes pleased with himself and with what he does—

> Little Jack Horner
> Sat in the corner,
> Eating of Christmas pie:
> He put in his thumb,
> And pulled out a plum,
> And said, "What a good boy am I!"

There are a lot of church members who are pulling out a plum and saying, "God surely must want to pat me on the head for what I am doing!"

The fourth question the people of Israel ask is going the limit: "Shall I give my firstborn for my transgression, the fruit of my body for the sin of my soul?" This was very meaningful to these people because they were surrounded by pagan peoples who in their worship of Molech and Baal offered human sacrifices. There were instances when even Israel turned in this direction. Two of the most godless kings of the southern kingdom indulged in human sacrifices—old Ahaz and old Manasseh. These two godless men offered their own children as burnt offerings, but is that what God would ask?

I want to make it very clear that God never asked these people to offer a child as a human sacrifice. God did require that they give to Him the firstborn male of everything that was born to them, whether it be a cow, a sheep, an ox, or their son. But God made it very clear to them that He did not require human sacrifice.

There are many passages of Scripture on this, but I will have to confine myself to just a few which I feel are ample to illustrate my point. In the eighteenth chapter of Numbers, God gave to the people certain regulations and told them what He required of them. We read there, "Every thing that openeth the matrix in all flesh, which they bring unto the LORD, whether it be of men or beasts, shall be thine: nevertheless the firstborn of man shalt thou surely redeem, and the firstling of unclean beasts shalt thou redeem" (Num. 18:15). God claimed the firstborn, you see. God required that the firstborn male child belonged to Him, but redemption money, silver, was to be taken and paid for that firstborn. In other words, God would not accept a human sacrifice, and He also would not accept the sacrifice of an unclean animal. I think that is interesting—man is unclean.

We have the practice today of dedicating our children to the Lord, and I think that that is a very fine thing to do. It has been my privilege to dedicate several thousand children in my days as a pastor. Some of them have turned out wonderfully well. One mother brought her son to me at a seminary where I was speaking, and she said, "Dr. McGee, you dedicated him when he was an infant." I thank the Lord that he has turned out well, but I have also dedicated some who have wound up in some of our best jails. It is nice to dedicate your child to the Lord, but that does not guarantee that he will turn out well.

In the Old Testament, God said, "You're to redeem the child, put up redemption money for him. I will not take him now." Why? He is like that unclean animal; he's unclean. That is the reason that a woman who had brought a child into the world was unclean—she had brought an unclean thing into the world. David said, "Behold, I was shapen in iniquity, and in sin did my mother conceive me" (Ps. 51:5). God doesn't want a child until he is redeemed. We are going to have to wait until our child has received Jesus Christ as his Savior; when he does that, God can take that child and use him. God will not take him and use him until then.

In Exodus we read, "Sanctify unto me all the firstborn, whatsoever openeth the womb among the children of Israel, both of man and of beast: it is mine" (Exod. 13:2). But then in Leviticus we find: "And thou shalt not let any of thy seed pass through the fire to Molech, neither shalt thou profane the name of thy God: I am the LORD" (Lev. 18:21). In other words, God said, "Do not offer a human sacrifice. Do not take your child and offer him as a human sacrifice. You would profane Me if you did that."

People say to me, "I surely hope that your little grandson is going to follow in your footsteps and become a preacher. I am praying that he will do that." I do not mean to be coldhearted, but I do not pray that way about my grandsons. In the best way that I can as a grandfather, I lift them to the Lord, and I have told the Lord that first of all I want them to be saved. Then I pray that the Lord will use them in whatever way He wills. If it is His will for one of them to be a pharmacist and roll pills, that would tickle me to death. If it is the Lord's will for one to dig ditches, I'm going to be for that. You and I cannot take a little child who has our fallen nature and force him into Christian service. It simply won't work; that's not the way it is done, if you please.

He hath shewed thee, O man, what is good; and what doth the LORD require of thee, but to do justly, and to love mercy, and to walk humbly with thy God? [Mic. 6:8].

Verse 8 is the joy and delight of liberals because they think that it presents a works religion, that it teaches that man can be saved by his works. What Micah is doing here is answering the questions of many sincere people in the northern kingdom of Israel who were in darkness, who had not been taught the Word of God. They wanted to know how to come before God. They wanted to know whether they should bring burnt offerings, whether they should bring many offerings, and whether they should offer even their own children as human sacrifices. Micah answers all of these questions: None of these things does God require. External religion without an internal experience, without reality on the inside, is absolutely valueless. There must be a rebirth, a new nature given to the individual. Externalities are not important—God never begins there. If you want to know what God takes delight in, what He requires of man, this verse will tell you. I want us to consider this verse carefully and in detail. Mr. Liberal, I insist that you interpret this accurately, and when you do, you will find that you are not saved by your good works because you do not *have* any good works.

"He hath shewed thee, O man, what is good." We notice first of all that this is addressed to *man*. This means not only the man in Israel but also the man in the United States, not only the person of the seventh century B.C. but also the person of the twentieth century A.D. This is for mankind.

These are the three things that God requires: (1) You are "to do justly"—that is, you must have a righteousness to present to God, you must be a righteous person. You are to be just in your dealings with your fellow man; you are to be honest and true. (2) You are "to love mercy." You are not only to love the mercy of God but also to be merciful in your own dealings with others. And (3) you are "to walk humbly with thy God."

How are you going to do these things, brother? Can you do them in your own strength? Do you think that you can do them without God's help? Do you think that you can do them without God's salvation? If you do, (I'm going to say something very strong, but I'm far enough away from you that you cannot hit me), you are a hypocrite! Don't tell me that you live by this moral code without the power of God. You cannot, for the very simple reason that all of these are the fruit of the Holy Spirit. "But the fruit of the Spirit is love, joy, peace, longsuffering, gentleness, goodness, faith, meekness, temperance: against such there is no law" (Gal. 5:22–23). All three of these things which Micah lists are the work of the Holy Spirit in the life of the believer. None of us has any one of these things in his life today.

Let's turn to the New Testament and see what is said there concerning this. Listen to a man who lived under the Law. In the fifteenth chapter of Acts, when the apostles were deciding whether the Gentiles would have to keep the Law in order to be saved, Simon Peter stood up and said, "But we believe that through the grace of the Lord Jesus Christ we shall be saved, even as they" (Acts 15:11). Why did he say that? Because he had just said in Acts 15:10, "Now therefore why tempt ye God, to put a yoke upon the neck of the disciples, which neither our fathers nor we were able to bear?" Simon Peter said, "I lived under the law" (and I don't think he ever got very far away from it even after he was saved), "yet I did not measure up to it."

God has made this very clear through the words of the apostle Paul also: "For they that are after the flesh do mind the things of the flesh; but they that are after the Spirit the things of the Spirit. For to be carnally minded is death; but to be spiritually minded is life and peace. Because the carnal mind is enmity against God: for it is not subject to the law of God, neither indeed can be. *So then they that are in the flesh cannot please God.* But ye are not in the flesh, but in the Spirit, if so be that the Spirit of God dwell in you . . ." (Rom. 8:5–9, italics mine).

My friend, how does the Spirit of God dwell in you? The Lord Jesus said, ". . . Ye must be born again" (John 3:7). You must be born again by receiving Christ. "But as many as received him, to them gave he power [the right, the authority, the *exousian* power] to become the sons of God, even to them that believe on his name" (John 1:12).

In Romans 3:9–18 the apostle Paul sets before us the condition of man. He brings man before the judgment bar of God and shows that he is guilty. Then Paul takes man into the clinic of God and shows that he is sick, sick nigh unto death—in fact, he is ". . . *dead* in trespasses and sins" (Eph. 2:1, italics mine). No man, therefore, whoever he is, can present these things to God. God requires righteousness, but we cannot meet that standard. Paul says, ". . . There is none righteous, no, not one" (Rom. 3:10). Someone says, "Well, that is in the New Testament." My friend, all that Paul is doing in this section of Romans is quoting the Old Testament. In Psalm 14:1 we find, "The fool hath said in his heart, There is no God. They are corrupt, they have done abominable works, there is none that doeth good." This is what God says about you. But God also says that He requires righteousness. How are you going to be able to present it to Him, my friend?

Paul goes on to say in Romans 3:11: "There is none that understandeth, there is none that seeketh after God." In other words, there is none that acts even on the knowledge that he has. Do you, if you are not a Christian, really live up to your ideals? Have you attained the goal that you have set? Have you come to the plateau in life where you are satisfied with your living? May I say to you, none of us even act on the knowledge which we have—"there is none that seeketh after God." Again, this idea is found in the Old Testament in Psalm 14:2–3: "The Lord looked down from heaven upon the children of men, to see if there were any that did understand, and seek God. They are all gone aside, they are all together become filthy: there is none that doeth good, no, not one."

I could multiply from the Old Testament such statements again and again. Righteousness is what God requires, but the Old Testament makes it very obvious that we cannot present our righteousness to God—because we don't have any. Since God requires righteousness, there must be a change in the life because there is none righteous. We are told that Jesus was ". . . delivered for our offences, and was raised again for our *justification*" (Rom. 4:25, italics mine). The Lord Jesus was raised for our righteousness, that we might have righteousness, that by the Spirit of God we might produce righteousness in our lives.

The "love of mercy"—we do not have that in our human hearts. We are dead in trespasses and sins. Paul says, "They are all gone out of the way, they are together become unprofitable; there is none that doeth good, no, not one" (Rom. 3:12). This is the picture of man; this is the way that man is today. The same point is presented to us by Isaiah: "All we like sheep have gone astray; we have turned every one to his own way; and the Lord hath laid on him the iniquity of us all" (Isa. 53:6). Evidently, "us all" have iniquity, or Isaiah would not have made a statement like that.

Therefore, let's not be hypocritical when we come to this verse in Micah that tells us that we are to walk humbly with our God. None seeketh after God; instead, we want to come to Him our way.

I want to say this in all kindness, but I trust that it might startle some and awaken them out of their condition today. If you believe that your church membership or your character or your good works are going to get you to God, then may I say that you are bypassing God's way. The Lord Jesus said, ". . . I am the way, the truth, and the life: no man cometh unto the Father, but by me" (John 14:6). If you can get to God by this route presented here—by doing justly, by loving mercy, and by walking humbly with God—and you can do that on your own, when you get to heaven, you can tell God to move over. You can tell Him that you want to share His throne with Him, that you got there by yourself, that you didn't need Him since you are your own god. But, my friend, God says that He does not share His glory with another, and I do not think He will share His throne with you. So why don't you come God's way and not man's way?

Doing justly, loving mercy, and walking humbly with God are things which God requires. Who are you kidding when you claim that you do these things in your natural state? My, how verses like this, when held up to the human family, show us what we really are like! Some commend themselves for being polite and nice folk, especially on Sundays when they seem so genteel and loving—and yet they have never come to God *His* way. How can you continue on and on in a hypocrisy like that? Why not be honest with God? Just come right out with it, go to Him, and tell Him that you are a sinner. He already knows it, but it would be nice if you told Him. Instead of climbing onto a psychiatrist's couch and talking to him, talk to God. Tell Him the thing that is wrong with you. Tell Him about your hangups. Tell Him about the sin in your life. God wants to save you, my friend. God wants to forgive your sins and give you the righteousness of Christ.

Having presented to these people what God requires, Micah is now going to show them how far they have fallen short of it. The reason that God will judge them is because of their willful and continual sinning.

The LORD's voice crieth unto the city, and the man of wisdom shall see thy name: hear ye the rod, and who hath appointed it [Mic. 6:9].

"The LORD's voice crieth unto the city." We have seen that Micah has been directing his prophecies largely to the urban areas, to the cities. His writing reveals that he is a very sophisticated writer. He was in the know; he belonged to the upper echelon. He is in contrast to Amos who said, "I'm no prophet. I'm just a gatherer of sycamore fruit. I'm a farmhand, just a country boy who has come to town." But Amos happened to be God's man. Micah is God's man too, but a different type of man from Amos—he is crying to the city.

"And the man of wisdom shall see thy name: hear ye the rod, and who hath appointed it." The rod is for judgment. We read in the second psalm, "Thou shalt break them with a rod of iron; thou shalt dash them in pieces like a potter's vessel" (Ps. 2:9). The rod represents the judgment of God. Judgment is coming upon this nation. The man of wisdom—that is, the man in that day who believed God and who would listen—would recognize that judgment was coming upon the nation and would act accordingly. The voice of God is lifted, and He speaks forth in judgment. The man is a wise man who sees the dealings of God which reveal His righteous character as well as the fact that he is longsuffering, patient, and will pardon iniquity. But God also punishes, and the rod is the badge of His authority as the judge who *will* judge.

There was still sin in the nation, and Micah is now going to reveal these sins specifically; he is going to spell them out.

> Are there yet the treasures of wickedness in the house of the wicked, and the scant measure that is abominable? [Mic. 6:10].

"Treasures of wickedness" refers to the wealth they had accumulated in their unjust dealings.

> Shall I count them pure with the wicked balances, and with the bag of deceitful weights? [Mic. 6:11].

Many of these people were coming into the temple, bringing a sacrifice, going through the outward ceremony, and saying that they were doing justly and loving mercy. But what were they doing during the week? God says, "Shall I count them pure with the wicked balances?" I tell you, the butchers in that day were weighing their thumbs—and some butchers had thumbs worth several drachmas! Businessmen were dishonest in their business dealings. He says, "And with the bag

of deceitful weights?" They were absolutely crooked. They were ava-
ricious, they were covetous, and they were greedy; yet they tried to
pass themselves off as religious folk.

**For the rich men thereof are full of violence, and the in-
habitants thereof have spoken lies, and their tongue is
deceitful in their mouth [Mic. 6:12].**

The rich were guilty of violence; they were liars. They were deceitful—you could not believe them.

Is this not a picture today of my own nation? Is this not a picture of
this wonderful land in which you and I live? We cannot believe the
news media today. We cannot believe the politicians, no matter what
their party affiliation. It's a day when it is difficult to believe businessmen. It is difficult to believe those in the military leadership. We are
living in a nation today where most of us little folk are confused—we
don't know whom to believe. This was the situation in Israel in Micah's day, and God did not approve of it. In fact, this is one of the
things that brought the nation down and brought the judgment of God
upon them.

I want to say this very carefully but clearly because I love my country and I hate to see what is happening to it today. I have taught for
years that the United States would have to go down at the end of this
age for the very simple reason that we are not mentioned in Bible
prophecy. We are a world power today, but will we be tomorrow? It
seems that we are going down very fast. At the time that I am writing
this, things look very dark in this land. An energy crisis has come
upon us. It didn't come suddenly; it has been coming for many years.
A few of us have been crying out that America is going to be judged.
We are apparently moving into that orbit today. Many warned years
ago after World War II that oil should have been brought out of the
Middle East at that time and that we should never have used our own
reserves. But because of greed (it was called "good business" because
it was making money), we went into an age of affluence and plenty,
and we really left God out. And He is pretty much left out of our na-
tional affairs today. There has been no mention, at the time that I am

writing this, that we need to turn to God in this emergency in which we find ourselves.

The northern kingdom of Israel in Micah's day was in the same condition in which we are today, and God brought judgment upon them. Although they were His chosen people as a nation, He brought judgment upon them.

> **Therefore also will I make thee sick in smiting thee, in making thee desolate because of thy sins [Mic. 6:13].**

In effect, God says, "First of all, I am going to start taking the oil away from you, but I'm not going to stop there. You're going to find that you will run short on many things before I am through judging you."

> **Thou shalt eat, but not be satisfied; and thy casting down shall be in the midst of thee; and thou shalt take hold, but shalt not deliver; and that which thou deliverest will I give up to the sword [Mic. 6:14].**

God says in effect, "You will no longer be able to enjoy all of these things that you have enjoyed, all these little goodies that you have had. Shortages and eventual famine will come. Attempts to remove your wealth to a safe place will be fruitless—the enemy will get it."

> **Thou shalt sow, but thou shalt not reap; thou shalt tread the olives, but thou shalt not anoint thee with oil; and sweet wine, but shalt not drink wine [Mic. 6:15].**

The enemy would take them from their land—take them to Assyria as captives.

God intended to cut them down but to cut them down gradually. That, of course, would give them an opportunity to turn to Him. The next chapter will make it clear that God would have pardoned them anytime that they would have turned to Him. But, my friend, you must turn to Him, for God will judge sin.

The people of Israel were going through the externalities of religion, but internally they were far from God. There was dishonesty in their business dealings. There was impurity in their lives. There was violence. There was lying and deceit. Every kind of flagrant sin was committed. And God cannot bless a people or a nation that engages in these things.

> For the statutes of Omri are kept, and all the works of the house of Ahab, and ye walk in their counsels; that I should make thee a desolation, and the inhabitants thereof an hissing: therefore ye shall bear the reproach of my people [Mic. 6:16].

A question would naturally be asked by a new reader of this: "Who in the world is Omri, and who in the world is Ahab? I have never heard of them before. Why is God saying what He is saying about them?" Such a question demonstrates the need for a different approach to the study of the Old Testament which I have for many years thought would be most helpful. I would suggest that when you study the historical books of the Old Testament, also consider the prophetic book or books that correspond to the same time period as the historical book. For example, that would mean that Micah should be studied along with the historical account of the reigns of Hezekiah in the southern kingdom and of Ahab and Jezebel in the northern kingdom. If the historical books were considered along with the prophetic books, they would give you a complete picture. I had hoped to introduce this approach when I was head of the English Bible department at the Bible Institute of Los Angeles years ago, but I never got around to it.

However, if we will now turn to the historical book of 1 Kings, it will shed some light on this verse here in Micah. Omri was one of the kings in the northern kingdom; in fact, he was one of the meanest. Omri and Zimri, then Tibni, reigned as rival kings until both died, and Omri prevailed to rule over the entire northern kingdom. In 1 Kings 16:24 we read: "And he bought the hill Samaria of Shemer for two talents of silver, and built on the hill, and called the name of the city which he built, after the name of Shemer, owner of the hill, Samaria." That city is called Samaria to this day, and the ruins of the city which Omri built are still there. But Omri is not really the one who developed the city. After the death of Omri, Ahab came to the throne. We read further: "So Omri slept with his fathers, and was buried in Samaria: and Ahab his son reigned in his stead. . . . And Ahab the son of Omri did evil in the sight of the LORD above all that were before him" (1 Kings 16:28, 30). Now that was something, let me tell you, but one of the reasons he was able to do that was because he had a great little helper in his wife, Jezebel. "And it came to pass, as if it had been a light thing for him to walk in the sins of Jeroboam the son of Nebat, that he took to wife Jezebel the daughter of Ethbaal king of the Zidonians, and went and served Baal, and worshipped him" (1 Kings 16:31). Ahab and Jezebel made the worship of Baal the religion of Israel!

"The statutes of Omri are kept, and all the works of the house of Ahab." Instead of following the statutes of the Lord, they followed the statutes of Omri and Ahab. They rejected the Word of the Lord and walked in their counsels instead. Now in Micah's day, almost two hundred years later, the effect and influence of their evil reigns are apparent.

We see the same effect evident in our own day. The leadership of any nation, if that nation is to prosper under God, must be godly. People like to criticize Queen Victoria and the Victorian Era in England— even the English ridicule it. However, I think it should be said that that happens to have been the greatest period in their history—that is when they had an empire. Victoria was Empress of India; she ruled an empire. Today Great Britain has really been cut down to size, for their leadership since then has not been what it should have been.

When Princess Anne was married, I rejoiced in watching the ceremony. Tears came into our eyes as my wife and I watched it on television, for in the ceremony there was a restoration of the sacredness of marriage. Since that example came from the leadership, I am sure that it had an influence.

My own country has not had a very good example set by either the White House or the Congress in a long, long time. My lifetime pretty much spans this century, and may I say, the example emanating from Washington has not been good. As a result, gross immorality has spread throughout this nation. I do believe, because of this verse here, that God would say that He holds the leaders of our nation during this century responsible for plunging the country into gross immorality through the example which they have set.

Micah presents God's philosophy of government. This is not being taught in any of our universities—that is part of our problem also. As a result, we're not really getting the facts, and our nation continues to decay and deteriorate. We will continue to do so unless a great revival should come to our land, but there is certainly no evidence at the present time that it will come.

CHAPTER 7

THEME: Pardoning all iniquity because of who God is and what He does; closing prayer; God's answer; paean of praise

PARDONING ALL INIQUITY BECAUSE OF WHO GOD IS AND WHAT HE DOES

In the first nine verses of chapter 7, the prophet Micah confesses that God is accurate in His complaint against Israel. The charge and the accuracy of it touch the heart of the prophet. He is not unfeeling. He is moved and motivated by the judgment which is coming upon his people. We have in this first section, therefore, a soliloquy of sorrow, a saga of suffering, a wail of woe, an elegy of eloquent grief.

> Woe is me! for I am as when they have gathered the summer fruits, as the grapegleanings of the vintage: there is no cluster to eat: my soul desired the firstripe fruit [Mic. 7:1].

Micah begins in a very personal way—he says, "Woe is me!" He is not only very personal, but he is also affected a great deal by God's message which he has relayed, just as Jeremiah was. He is overwhelmed by it. He is grieved by it. He finds no delight in saying these things. There is no fun today in my saying things that are rather pessimistic about the United States. A great many people will not agree with me about them. They will rebuke me for not being patriotic and for not showing a love for my country. My friend, I love my country as much as the normal American loves his country. I find no joy in saying these things. I wish that I could make an announcement to say, "Friends, a great revival is breaking out across this land!" That would be good news, and that would be wonderful, but I just have to say along with Micah, "Woe is me!"

"For I am as when they have gathered the summer fruits, as the

grapegleanings of the vintage: there is no cluster to eat: my soul desired the firstripe fruit." Remember that in Scripture the vine is used
to picture the nation Israel. Micah's contemporary, Isaiah, is the one
who enlarged upon this and set this forth (see Isa. 5). He said very
clearly that Israel is the vine and the vine is Israel. Micah looked about
at his nation and said, "I've looked for a good cluster of grapes, and
there are none on the vine. I desired the firstripe fruit, and there was
none. The vine is not producing fruit."

Micah is going to deal now with the specifics—

**The good man is perished out of the earth: and there is
none upright among men: they all lie in wait for blood;
they hunt every man his brother with a net [Mic. 7:2].**

It is not safe to walk on the streets of our country—today lawlessness
abounds. It does seem that the good man is perished; yet there are a
lot of wonderful people left in this nation of ours. I am sure there were
godly people left in Israel also, but Micah is speaking generally. The
good man is not the ideal, and he's not the one in the majority. "The
good man is perished out of the earth."

**That they may do evil with both hands earnestly, the
prince asketh, and the judge asketh for a reward; and
the great man, he uttereth his mischievous desire: so
they wrap it up [Mic. 7:3].**

"That they may do evil with both hands earnestly." They are not satisfied to do evil in just a minor way with one hand—they are going at it
with both hands. Believe me, doing evil really kept them busy.

"The prince asketh, and the judge asketh for a reward." They were
doing evil for a reward. They were not only willing to stoop to do the
thing that was wrong, but they did it also because of greed and covetousness on their part. "The prince . . . and the judge"—there was
crookedness in government, you see. You would expect the prince
and the judge to rule justly and righteously, but that was not the picture.

"And the great man, he uttereth his mischievous desire." The writers of our literature are clever writers today. I watch a great deal of television in order to keep up with what is going on in this world. I find that everything that is presented by our writers has a little hook in it. There's that little hook of liberalism, that little hook of immorality, that little hook of ridicule of the things we have considered sacred in this country. And it is all done in the name of the sacred cow of the freedom of the press and the freedom of speech. But there is very little freedom of religion today, unless it is weird and way out in left field somewhere and not that which is Bible-centered and Bible-anchored. We need a bibliocentric thrust in this nation of ours today.

> **The best of them is as a brier: the most upright is sharper than a thorn hedge: the day of thy watchmen and thy visitation cometh; now shall be their perplexity [Mic. 7:4].**

Even the best people were like a brier—you had to be careful. You can get stuck with a brier, you know, if you're not careful with it. That was the condition of even the best people in Micah's day—you couldn't depend on them. "The best of them is as a brier: the most upright is sharper than a thorn hedge."

Our writers are clever and sophisticated today, but we have no geniuses writing, just clever boys. They write clever plays. They say clever things. They write clever articles. But there are no geniuses. They write nothing of depth, nothing that is actually worthwhile. I believe that God will do with our contemporary culture what He did with Israel in that day and what He did later on with the Greek and Roman cultures. He simply wiped them off the face of the earth. Why preserve it? What is being done today that has eternal value? Oh, my friend, what a parallel there is here, and how accurate Micah is!

"The day of thy watchmen and thy visitation cometh; now shall be their perplexity." The Lord Jesus said, "And there shall be signs in the sun, and in the moon, and in the stars; and upon the earth distress of nations, with perplexity; the sea and the waves roaring" (Luke 21:25). In other words, one thing that would characterize the end of the age is perplexity of nations, confusion of nations. The biggest sign that we are near the end of the age is not found in Israel. Israel is not a sign. We are living in the church age today. We don't need to look for a day, we need to look at a weather report: the sea and the waves roaring, the storms breaking upon the earth, and the nations seething—that is the picture that God's Word presents of the nation in the last days.

Micah has been telling about the difficulty that these people were having, the sin that was in their lives. The lovely statement that was made back in Micah 6:8 was: "He hath shewed thee, O man, what is good; and what doth the LORD require of thee, but to do justly, and to love mercy, and to walk humbly with thy God?" The people just were not doing it, and they found that they could not do it. As Peter said, "We were under the yoke of the law. Our forefathers didn't keep it, and we cannot keep it today" (see Acts 15:10). Yet there are a great many people going to church, thinking they are saved by their own good works and are acceptable to God on the basis of what they do. There is no hypocrisy like that kind of hypocrisy! The people living back yonder under the Law might be excused for thinking that, but we have an open Bible which makes clear to us that we are saved only by the grace of God.

> **Trust ye not in a friend, put ye not confidence in a guide: keep the doors of thy mouth from her that lieth in thy bosom [Mic. 7:5].**

This reveals something of the awful condition that existed in that day, and it has been true pretty much of all the so-called civilizations of this world. It is a big, mean world outside. We need to recognize this, especially if we are to take a stand for God. The Lord Jesus said, "Think not that I am come to send peace on earth: I came not to send peace, but a sword" (Matt. 10:34). As long as there is evil in the world there will be a conflict and a war between that which is of the flesh and that which is of the Spirit, between light and darkness, between good and evil.

I generally get up very early in the morning because I like to do my studying at home early. I get up while it is still dark, and my study is where I can look out toward the east. It is interesting to watch how the darkness wrestles with the light until finally the sun comes bursting over the horizon and the darkness then vanishes. There is always that period of dawn when it would seem that the darkness is wrestling with the light. The same thing takes place in the evening at dusk when again darkness wants to take over. There is that kind of a *spiritual* struggle going on in the world.

The Lord Jesus went on to say in Matthew, "For I am come to set a man at variance against his father, and the daughter against her mother, and the daughter-in-law against her mother-in-law. And a man's foes shall be they of his own household" (Matt. 10:35–36). You will not be able to trust your own family. Micah says, "Trust ye not in a friend, put ye not confidence in a guide: keep the doors of thy mouth from her that lieth in thy bosom." Over the years I have heard of many such instances—and it works both ways, of course—when a wife has not been able to trust her husband, and a husband has not been able to trust his wife.

We live in a day when the word of man seems to carry less value than it ever has before. You cannot believe what you read, and you cannot believe what you hear on radio or on television. The child of God should test everything. I say this very candidly: test every radio program you listen to by the Word of God. Test my Bible-teaching broadcast; test them all. You will be wise if you do this because the human nature is not to be trusted.

For the son dishonoureth the father, the daughter riseth up against her mother, the daughter-in-law against her mother-in-law; a man's enemies are the men of his own house [Mic. 7:6].

Notice that this is exactly what the Lord Jesus said will come, and it had come in Micah's day also. When this sort of a situation arises, it is a day of decadence, a day of deterioration, a day of decay. It is a day that is very dark, by the way. We live in a day like that. We have gotten to the place where government is having to watch everything. But who is going to watch government? They need watching also. Whom can you trust? In whom can you believe today? We are living at a very sad time in the history of the world. This verse reveals the condition of that day of Micah's grief. This is not something to boast of, not something to rejoice in. It is something to be deplored, something which should grieve your heart and my heart.

Therefore I will look unto the LORD; I will wait for the God of my salvation: my God will hear me [Mic. 7:7].

We see here the confidence and the assurance and the faith of Micah. He knows that God is going to hear him, and he knows that God will work this thing out. The Lord Jesus said that there would be distress of nations, the sea and the waves would roar, and the nations of the world would be in great turmoil. But it does not matter how dark it is today and how high the waves are rolling—these things ought not to disturb the child of God, they ought not to detour us. For the Lord Jesus said, "Men's hearts [will be] failing them for fear, and for looking after those things which are coming on the earth: for the powers of heaven shall be shaken. . . . And when these things begin to come to pass, then look up, and lift up your heads; for your redemption draweth nigh" (Luke 21:26, 28). Micah says, "Therefore I will look unto the LORD; I will wait for the God of my salvation: my God will hear me." These are the days when God's children need to stay very close to God, and we need to stay close to the Word of God.

Rejoice not against me, O mine enemy: when I fall, I shall arise; when I sit in darkness, the LORD shall be a light unto me [Mic. 7:8].

This is a great principle that we find running through the Scriptures. Though God's man may fall, God will raise him up. When we sit in darkness, the Lord shall be a light for us. God's people, again may I repeat this, must stay close to the Word of God in dark and difficult days.

Now in verse 9, on behalf of his people, Micah makes a confession to God, or as The New Scofield Reference Bible has labeled it, "submission to the LORD." There is sweet submission here and, in spite of the darkness, there is on his lips a praise to God. He has just said to the enemy, "Don't you rejoice against me. God is going to lift me up, and then I will be able to rejoice. Though I sit in darkness, the Lord is going to be a light unto me." Micah had the confidence that God would deliver him and would deliver his people.

> **I will bear the indignation of the LORD, because I have sinned against him, until he plead my cause, and execute judgment for me: he will bring me forth to the light, and I shall behold his righteousness [Mic. 7:9].**

Micah is making a public confession of the sin of the people. What confidence this man has! He submits himself to the will of God. That should be the position of every child of God in this dark hour in the history of the world. What is it that we should do? Well, there is one thing that is sure: God has permitted all things to happen, and He is still in control. Therefore we should submit ourselves to God. We should confess our sins and keep our accounts with God right up to date and make sure that we have settled every account with Him. This is the thing that is all-important.

Notice that Micah says, "I will bear the indignation of the LORD." Why? "Because I have sinned against him." My friend, we as a nation have sinned. You have sinned; I have sinned. We have gone along with this affluent society and have accepted its comforts. We have rather smiled at the lack of integrity that there is in public life, and we have shut our eyes to the gross immorality that is around us. It is time that some of us are confessing our sin.

"Until he plead my cause, and execute judgment for me." God will use the "rod" of Assyria to punish His children for their sins, but afterward He will restore them and bring them "forth to the light." Then they will "behold his righteousness"—they will realize that God was just in punishing them.

> **Then she that is mine enemy shall see it, and shame shall cover her which said unto me, Where is the LORD**

thy God? mine eyes shall behold her: now shall she be
trodden down as the mire of the streets [Mic. 7:10].

God will ultimately triumph, but the thing that is tragic is that, because of the sins of the people, they must be judged. Their enemy asks
the question: "You boasted of the fact that you serve God, but where is
He? Why doesn't He help you? Why doesn't He deliver you? You have
said that He would." Well, the enemy could not see the righteousness
of God. He did not see that God was dealing with His people in a
righteous way by judging them.

After God restores His people, He will punish the nations that
abused them and attempted to annihilate them—then they shall "be
trodden as the mire of the streets."

Since the Assyrian captivity lay ahead of the people of Israel, the
"enemy" is interpreted as the nation of Assyria; yet the following two
verses indicate that a later and final enemy is also in view.

Micah has predicted the destruction of Israel's enemies and now
turns to Israel's restoration. The nation of Israel is likened to a vineyard in several passages of Scripture. Notice especially Isaiah's song
of the vineyard (see Isa. 5:1–7). The walls Micah speaks of are the
walls around a vineyard.

**In the day that thy walls are to be built, in that day shall
the decree be far removed [Mic. 7:11].**

In the early days of their history, the people of Israel were sent by God
down to Egypt to become a nation. Then God hedged them into the
land of Palestine, gave them the Law, made them a peculiar people,
and kept them from intermarrying with other folk. Then, because of
their sin, God sent them into Assyrian and Babylonian captivity. They
had a ministry to the world, both at the time of the containment and
then again when they were scattered throughout the world.

**In that day also he shall come even to thee from Assyria,
and from the fortified cities, and from the fortress even**

to the river, and from sea to sea, and from mountain to
mountain [Mic. 7:12].

As we have seen in chapter 4, during the millennial Kingdom all nations shall come to Zion—even their former enemy, Assyria. "And
many nations shall come, and say, Come, and let us go up to the
mountain of the LORD, and to the house of the God of Jacob; and he will
teach us of his ways, and we will walk in his paths: for the law shall
go forth of Zion, and the word of the LORD from Jerusalem" (Mic. 4:2).

However, Micah reminds them that before this time of blessing,
punishment lies before them.

**Notwithstanding the land shall be desolate because of
them that dwell therein, for the fruit of their doings
[Mic. 7:13].**

You see, the land and the people are pretty well tied together. That
land was not always desolate as it is today. When the blessing of God
comes upon the people, it will also come again upon that land—but it
has not yet come upon them.

CLOSING PRAYER

Now Micah in a very wonderful way commits his people to the Shepherd's care—

**Feed thy people with thy rod, the flock of thine heritage,
which dwell solitarily in the wood, in the midst of Carmel: let them feed in Bashan and Gilead, as in the days
of old [Mic. 7:14].**

"Feed thy people with thy rod, the flock of thine heritage." In Micah
6:9 the rod was a rod of judgment; here it is a rod of comfort. ". . . thy
rod and thy staff they comfort me" (Ps. 23:4). I think it simply refers to
the staff of the shepherd which could be used in two ways: it could be

used to protect and help the sheep, and it could also be used to discipline the sheep. "Feed thy people with thy rod"—God disciplines us, and He instructs us.

"Which dwell solitarily in the wood, in the midst of Carmel: let them feed in Bashan and Gilead, as in the days of old." These are great grazing lands up in the north and across the Jordan River.

Micah has come to God in beautiful submission and in confession of sin—confession of his sins and of the sins of the people. The prophets always identified themselves with the people in any confession of sin. (We do it a little differently; we like to confess the sin of the other fellow while we try to leave ours out.)

GOD'S ANSWER

God gives an answer to the prayer of the prophet. There has always been some question as to what this passage makes reference to, but it is the consensus of most expositors that it looks to the future and to the day when the Lord Jesus will come to set up His Kingdom.

> According to the days of thy coming out of the land of Egypt will I shew unto him marvellous things [Mic. 7:15].

God led Israel out of Egypt by miracle, but He did not bring them out of Babylon by miracle. No miracles are mentioned in connection with that, although their return to the land was a wonderful thing. It was the deliverance out of Egypt that was miraculous, and God says here that that will be the pattern for the day when He again brings them into the land. We have not seen anything like that in their present-day return to the land. We ought to recognize, therefore, that God has not yet fulfilled this prophecy.

> The nations shall see and be confounded at all their might: they shall lay their hand upon their mouth, their ears shall be deaf [Mic. 7:16].

When God begins again to move them back into the land, the world will stand in amazement, just as the peoples round about them did at the time of their exodus from Egypt. You remember the confession of the harlot, Rahab: "For we have heard how the LORD dried up the water of the Red sea for you, when ye came out of Egypt; and what ye did unto the two kings of the Amorites, that were on the other side Jordan, Sihon and Og, whom ye utterly destroyed. And as soon as we had heard these things, our hearts did melt, neither did there remain any more courage in any man, because of you: for the LORD your God, he is God in heaven above, and in earth beneath" (Josh. 2:10–11). The word has gotten around as to how God had taken care of His people.

> **They shall lick the dust like a serpent, they shall move out of their holes like worms of the earth: they shall be afraid of the LORD our God, and shall fear because of thee [Mic. 7:17].**

This refers to the godless nations which have attempted to destroy Israel. In that day when He comes to deliver Israel, "they shall be afraid of the LORD our God, and shall fear because of thee."

PAEAN OF PRAISE

Micah waxes eloquent now, and he asks a question—

> **Who is a God like unto thee, that pardoneth iniquity, and passeth by the transgression of the remnant of his heritage? he retaineth not his anger for ever, because he delighteth in mercy [Mic. 7:18].**

We will discuss this verse at length in a moment, but Micah goes on here to say that because of who God is, this is what He will do—

> **He will turn again, he will have compassion upon us; he will subdue our iniquities; and thou wilt cast all their sins into the depths of the sea.**

> **Thou wilt perform the truth to Jacob, and the mercy to Abraham, which thou hast sworn unto our fathers from the days of old [Mic. 7:19–20].**

Israel's sin put them out of the land temporarily, but God will make good His promises in spite of their sin. Their sin does not cancel out God's promises and God's covenant with these people any more than a child of God loses his salvation when he sins. His sin means that he is going to the woodshed for a good whipping if he doesn't confess it and get it straightened out; but if he will come back to God, God will graciously pardon him. The prodigal son did not get a whipping when he came home to his father; he got his whipping in the far country. And you can be sure of one thing: God's child will never be able to get by with sin. We see that again and again in Scripture.

Now let's come back to this marvelous statement that we have here: "Who is a God like unto thee." I want to make a very startling statement: There is something that God has not seen but which you see every day. Perhaps you didn't know that you could see something that God cannot see—but that is a true statement. It may sound rather impertinent for me to say that; it may sound irrelevant, irreverent, or inappropriate; it may even sound flippant or facetious. It may sound to you like I am making a parody or a pun, a riddle or a rhyme, a trick or a treat, but I want to assure you that this is a serious and sober subject with a sensible and Scriptural answer. The prophet here asks a profound question: "Who is a God like unto thee?" And it demands a thoughtful answer. The very nature of the question suggests an answer to an enigmatic subject.

This is not the first time in Scripture that this question has been asked, by the way. It was asked in that wonderful song sung by Israel after they crossed the Red Sea. In Exodus 15:11 we read, "Who is like unto thee, O Lord, among the gods? who is like thee, glorious in holiness, fearful in praises, doing wonders?" The people had just come out from Egypt where there were many gods. Egypt was absolutely—if I may use the slang expression—lousy with idols; they had many gods and many lords. The ten plagues in Egypt had been leveled at their various gods—that was God's strategy in it all. And then again at the end of the forty years of the wilderness march, Moses said, "There is none like unto the God of Jeshurun, who rideth upon the heaven in thy help, and in his excellency on the sky. The eternal God is thy refuge, and underneath are the everlasting arms: and he shall thrust out the enemy from before thee; and shall say, Destroy them" (Deut. 33:26–27). This question was again asked by Solomon in 1 Kings 8:23, ". . . Lord God of Israel, there is no God like thee, in heaven above, or on earth beneath, who keepest covenant and mercy with thy servants that walk before thee with all their heart." The psalmist exclaimed: "Who is like unto the Lord our God, who dwelleth on high, who humbleth himself to behold the things that are in heaven, and in the earth!" (Ps. 113:5–6).

This question is asked in Exodus, Deuteronomy, Kings, Psalms, and in other passages which I have not cited, but now let's answer it. The answer was suggested by my statement at the beginning: God has not seen something which you see every day. What is it that God has not seen? My friend, God has not seen His equal. "Who is a God like unto thee?" God has never seen His equal, but you and I see our equals every day.

There are many ways in which God is alone, in which God is unequaled. Only one of them is suggested by our passage here in Micah, but because this is such a profound question and one that is so basic to this book, I want to look at this subject closely: Who is a God like unto our God?

1. *The God of the Bible is the Creator.* The God of the Bible is the Creator, but the gods of the heathen are creatures. The apostle Paul wrote: "Because that, when they knew God, they glorified him not as God, neither were thankful; but became vain in their imaginations, and their foolish heart was darkened. Professing themselves to be wise, they became fools, And changed the glory of the uncorruptible God into an image made like to corruptible man, and to birds, and fourfooted beasts, and creeping things" (Rom. 1:21–23). They worshiped the creature rather than the Creator.

Isaiah, Micah's contemporary, wrote concerning the heathen who make images from trees: "He burneth part thereof in the fire; with part thereof he eateth flesh; he roasteth roast, and is satisfied: yea, he warmeth himself, and saith, Aha, I am warm, I have seen the fire: and the residue thereof he maketh a god, even his graven image: he falleth down unto it, and worshippeth it, and prayeth unto it, and saith, Deliver me; for thou art my god" (Isa. 44:16–17). Isaiah went on to say, "Remember these, O Jacob and Israel; for thou art my servant: I have formed thee; thou art my servant: O Israel, thou shalt not be forgotten of me" (Isa. 44:21). God is the Creator.

You may say, "But we don't have idols today." The Book of Micah has been dealing with a form of idolatry of which Israel was guilty and of which we are guilty also: covetousness is idolatry. Secularism, materialism, that to which you give yourself is your god. That which takes your time and your money is your god. It can be pleasure, it can be sex, it can be money—whatever you are giving yourself to, my friend, is your god. It does not matter what church you might belong to, whatever you are giving yourself to is your god.

With biting irony, God asks the question through the prophet Isaiah: "To whom will ye liken me, and make me equal, and compare me, that we may be like?" (Isa. 46:5). He is the Creator—you cannot make a picture of Him. "They lavish gold out of the bag, and weigh silver in the balance, and hire a goldsmith; and he maketh it a god: they fall down, yea, they worship. They bear him upon the shoulder, they carry him . . ." (Isa. 46:6–7). The supreme question is this: Is your religion carrying you, or are you carrying it? Many people say to me, "Oh, I find Christian work extremely boring. It is hard; it is difficult." If you are finding it that way, then I would suggest that you give up what you are doing—quit teaching your Sunday school class, quit singing in the choir, and do not be an officer in the church. If it is burdensome to you, He does not want you to do it. He doesn't want you carrying Him around—He wants to carry you. He wants to carry all of His children. Somebody said to me the other day, "Why in the world don't you retire? You are in your seventies now, you've been in the pastorate for forty years, and you've given your time to teaching the Bible on radio. Why don't you retire?" Do you want to know something? I would rather teach the Word of God than eat ice cream any day. I'd rather do this than eat a chicken dinner. My friend, God has been carrying me for a long time, even though I think I have been a heavy load for Him.

So God is unique; He is the Creator, and He carries us. "In the beginning God created the heaven and the earth" (Gen. 1:1)—and it is blasphemy to go beyond that. You cannot go beyond Him—". . . from everlasting to everlasting [from the vanishing point to the vanishing point], thou art God" (Ps. 90:2). He is the Creator.

2. *The God of the Bible is holy and righteous.* This is something that is very important to this little Book of Micah and to all sixty-six books of the Bible. God is a holy and righteous God. The gods of the heathen are little, they're contemptible, they're base, they're ignoble, they're shabby, they're evil, they're mean, and they're ugly—just think about the heathen images which you have seen. The gods of the Greeks on top of Mount Olympus were simply man's projection of himself. They were the enlargement of mankind. What did they do? They acted like overgrown children with overgrown faults and sins; they were spiteful and vengeful. The gods of the heathen are not pretty, my friend.

What a reflection and slur upon God! Have you ever noticed how many times in Scripture we read of "the *beauty* of holiness"? Oh, my friend, our God is beautiful—He is the beautiful one. Remember that He said to His people, ". . . thou thoughtest that I was altogether such an one as thyself . . ." (Ps. 50:21). He says, "I am not like you. You are sinful; you stoop to do low, mean things. I am holy; I am righteous." In Isaiah God says, "For my thoughts are not your thoughts, neither are your ways my ways . . ." (Isa. 55:8).

God is holy, and He says that He hates sin. He is angry with sin. He gets wrought-up over it, my friend. And the wrath of God must be revealed against sin. That is the reason judgment must come. There is no escape from it; there is no way out. The judgment of God is something that is going to come to pass.

Again the little Book of Micah has real application to my own nation today. This country has really been shaken in the past ten years. Consider this whole century and the things which have actually shaken this world in which you and I live. It is not the same world I was born into. I never dreamed that I would live to see the things which have taken place in my own days. What is back of all this? Well, our God is a holy God, and He reveals His anger against sin—He will judge it. I know that a judgment day is coming in the future for sinners who will not accept Christ, but God is moving today, and I believe that we are experiencing the anger of God.

A godless nation, a nation which rejects God, must bear the consequences. We must also recognize that as individuals you and I are sinners and must come to God. This is what it means to "walk humbly with thy God." You do not come to Him boasting of what you have done. You come to Him confessing. "I'm a sinner, and I need Your salvation." You must accept His salvation, recognizing that you could not go to heaven in your own righteousness. Anselm, one of the great thinkers of the eleventh century, wrote, "I would rather go to hell without sin than go to heaven with sin." That's a great statement. That will shake you, my friend. In this day of "weak tea" theology, we need to hear strong statements like this.

3. *The God of the Bible pardons iniquity and delights in mercy.* Verse 18 says, "Who is a God like unto thee, that pardoneth iniquity, and passeth by the transgression of the remnant of his heritage? he retaineth not his anger for ever, because he delighteth in mercy." Here is where our God is wonderfully and amazingly different. He has no equal here; there is no one even in His neighborhood.

". . . who is like thee, glorious in holiness, fearful in praises, doing wonders?" (Exod. 15:11). What are some of the wonders that God does? Read Exodus 33:18–19: "And he said, I beseech thee, shew me thy glory. And he said, I will make all my goodness pass before thee, and I will proclaim the name of the LORD before thee; and will be gracious to whom I will be gracious, and will shew mercy on whom I will shew mercy." God said, "Moses, I'm going to do this for you, not because you are Moses and the leader of My people, but I'm doing this because I am gracious, because I show mercy, and I do it for everybody." All you have to do is come to Him and claim His mercy, friend; He is just that good, and there is none like Him.

Again in Exodus we read: "And the LORD descended in the cloud, and stood with him there, and proclaimed the name of the LORD. And the LORD passed by before him, and proclaimed, The LORD, The LORD God, merciful and gracious, longsuffering, and abundant in goodness and truth, keeping mercy for thousands, forgiving iniquity and transgression and sin, and that will by no means clear the guilty . . ." (Exod. 34:5–7). My friend, how wonderful He is! God does not clear the guilty. "Wrong is wrong, from the moment it happens till the crack of doom," says the hero of the play, *The Great Divide*. All the angels in heaven working overtime cannot change that by a hair. But God can forgive the sinner and clear him of all charges because His holiness has been satisfied by Christ's vicarious death.

God's forgiveness is set forth in the Scripture by many figures of speech. I would like to mention just a few of them. His forgiveness is like a *debt* which has been paid. In Isaiah He says, "I, even I, am he that blotteth out thy transgressions for mine own sake, and will not remember thy sins" (Isa. 43:25). Peter said, "Repent ye therefore, and be converted, that your sins may be blotted out . . ." (Acts 3:19). On His ledger I am in debt, because there it is written, ". . . the wages of sin is death . . ." (Rom. 6:23), and ". . . in Adam all die . . ." (1 Cor. 15:22). God's forgiveness is set forth in Scripture as the healing of a *disease*. Jeremiah writes, "Return, ye backsliding children, and I will heal your backslidings . . ." (Jer. 3:22). And in Isaiah 61:1 He has promised to ". . . bind up the brokenhearted. . . ." Finally, God's forgiveness is pictured as the cleansing of a *pollution*, a *contamination*. The Scriptures tell us that ". . . according to his mercy he saved us, by the washing of regeneration, and renewing of the Holy Ghost" (Titus 3:5). And we read also, ". . . the blood of Jesus Christ his Son cleanseth us from all sin" (1 John 1:7). How wonderful our God is!

How does God forgive? God is different for there is none like Him in forgiving. His forgiveness is very different from yours and mine. If you step on my toe in a crowd, you turn to me and say, "Pardon me, will you forgive me?" I say, "Sure," but I'm thinking that, of course, you ought to give me the money to renew the shoeshine you have just ruined! But I say that I forgive you. Another example is a letter that I received some time ago from a man who confessed that he had been talking about me behind my back. Now he had found out that he was wrong, and he asked me to forgive him. I told him, "Don't ask me for forgiveness. Simply get it straightened out with the people you talked to and with the Lord." That's all I asked of him, because I had never known about it before I received his letter. Human forgiveness is pretty easy to come by.

However, God never forgives until the debt is paid. And on the Cross Christ paid the debt. He redeemed us. We are sold under sin. We today have offended the holiness of God. We are in debt to Him. We have a disease, and God is not going to take the disease of sin into heaven. But Christ paid our debt, and Christ is the One who will forgive us. He cleanses us, and He makes us acceptable in God's sight so that we might go to heaven someday.

"Who is a God like unto thee, that pardoneth iniquity, and passeth by the transgression of the remnant of his heritage? he retaineth not his anger for ever, because he delighteth in mercy." Isn't He a wonderful God? He is someday going to restore Israel to the land, not because they are wonderful, but because He is wonderful. And, my friend, I am going to heaven someday, but I am not going there because I am good or righteous—I am not. I'm going to heaven because Jesus died for me. I'm going because the debt has been paid, and there is no God like my God.

BIBLIOGRAPHY

(Recommended for Further Study)

Feinberg, Charles L. *The Minor Prophets*. Chicago, Illinois: Moody Press, 1976.

Gaebelein, Arno C. *The Annotated Bible*. 1917. Reprint. Neptune, New Jersey: Loizeaux Brothers, 1971.

Ironside, H. A. *The Minor Prophets*. Neptune, New Jersey: Loizeaux Brothers, n.d.

Jensen, Irving L. *Minor Prophets of Judah*. Chicago, Illinois: Moody Press, 1975. (Obadiah, Joel, Micah, Nahum, Zephaniah, and Habakkuk)

Tatford, Frederick A. *The Minor Prophets*. Minneapolis, Minnesota: Klock & Klock, n.d.

Unger, Merrill F. *Unger's Commentary on the Old Testament*, Vol. 2. Chicago, Illinois: Moody Press, 1982.